YOU KNOW ME ANTY NELLY?

To

OUR DEACEN BERNIE

FROM

ANN ROSE . PEGGY.

YOU KNOW ME ANTY NELLY?

LIVERPOOL CHILDREN'S RHYMES

COMPILED WITH NOTES ON
KIDS' GAMES AND LIVERPOOL LIFE

BY

FRANK SHAW

FOREWORD BY
PETER OPIE

1970
WOLFE PUBLISHING LTD
10 EARLHAM STREET · LONDON WC2

It is no reproach to the noblest of poetry to say that it is heard on the lips of the common people.—*German folklorist* HERDER.

Cover photograph by KARL HUGHES

This book was originally published in 1969 by The Gear Press. This is a revised and considerably enlarged edition.

Printed in Great Britain by C. Nicholls & Company Ltd.

CONTENTS

FOREWORD
By Peter Opie

THE myth that the English are a prim people, more inclined to propriety than passion, to Sunday silence than shrill silliness, to bellyaching than belly laughter, is as absurd today as it has always been; but it is easy to see how it arose. For generations we have held book-learning to be the sole requirement of our brightest pupils. We have hived off the learned from the unlearned, aborted the embryo poet from the body of the people, polished our intelligentsia so smooth they have no ear-flaps left to hear common speech and sentiment. And the intelligentsia, by vocation, are the people who project our image to the world at large.

Up to ten or twelve years ago, up to, let us say, the emergence of 'folk' as a recognised art form, cultured Englishmen tended to believe traditional speech and humour were almost extinct. They knew, of course, that vivid language had existed in Shakespeare's day because their universities had told them of it. They knew, from the memoirs of the mashers, that a costermonger-type of wit was current in Victorian days. But they had no knowledge of contemporary lore; and if it was suggested that oral rhyme and bright metaphor continued, as in the past, to be an English commonplace they replied—very rightly from their print-orientated point of view—'Where's the evidence?'

The 'folk' cult has brought a popular sub-culture into the open. But it has remained difficult for the literary critic to see its roots, and appreciate the liveliness of traditional rhyme. Ordinarily, when a trite oral verse is recorded on paper, or even on tape, its spirit is lost. Its magic evaporates. The humour of popular verse depends on nonchalance: the unexpectedness of somebody suddenly uttering words in rhyme instead of prose.

The Mersey banks
Was made for Yanks
And little girls like Ivy . . .

The sentiment doesn't bear a moment's reflection, and isn't
intended to, any more than a toffee paper dropped in the evening breeze. What if an Opie can trace the words back, via
Pantosfinx, to the Middle Ages? The speaker isn't concerned,
and the hearer isn't concerned, and the verse has probably
been only half-heard anyway. This is living literature, not an
examination paper. And the joy of *You Know Me Anty
Nelly* is that Frank Shaw conveys this nonchalance. He has, it
must be recognized, achieved a feat of considerable literary
difficulty.

Until recently almost all writers who have set out to record
some part of our oral lore have been outsiders: they have been
people who felt they were reporting something strange. They
have been antiquarians, or philologists, or mythologists,
people who seem to find it necessary to kill their material as
soon as they find it: scholar-maggots who can feed on a body
only when it is cool. The one literary craftsman who has
attempted to turn a collection of oral verses into a work of art
has been Norman Douglas; yet *London Street Games*, classic as
it is, today seems laboured, almost coy, compared with *Anty
Nelly*.

Of course Norman Douglas was not able to speak in the ver-
nacular, the way Frank Shaw does, so that rhyme and com-
mentary are almost indistinguishable, spoken in the same voice.
And Norman Douglas suffered from a further, more serious
disadvantage. He was well-versed in street lore, but he never
really understood it: where it came from, where it was going
to, how it was transmitted. He was convinced, for instance,
that the rhymes he was recording were local and ephemeral,
that they'd been made up by the children themselves, that they
would soon be forgotten. Frank Shaw is under no such illus-
ions. He knows his rhymes are Liverpool rhymes, yet he knows
most of them can also be picked up in London and Glasgow
and Belfast, and that this doesn't matter because if they'd been
collected in one of those cities they would, however subtly,

have been different. They wouldn't be these rhymes he's learned in the Pool.

Any rhyme that is alive in oral tradition is like all other living things, it is ever-evolving, it is both old and new at once. However seemingly commonplace a rhyme may be it is likely, also, to be unique. It is as common, almost, to find a diamond in a pot of scouse as two recordings of an oral rhyme that are identical. (I can tell in an instant when some writer has been purloining material I have collected.) One can say of a recording only that this is how it was known to a particular person, in a particular place, at a particular point in time.

You Know Me Anty Nelly is a collection of rhymes that are ordinary yet extraordinary. The book should be read, as Norman Douglas counselled his 'breathless catalogue' should be read, '*accelerando*, from beginning to end without a break'. In doing so something will be heard of the laughter and lilt of Liverpool, and something be caught as well, for this is no mean book, of the suffering and ebullience of mankind everywhere. But the individual rhymes, or their exact wording here, should be forgotten. We shouldn't pretend that they are little works of art, and rip them from their setting, and stuff them in anthologies. For if ever we become self-conscious or precious about our oral lore, if ever we start thinking—as bookish people are inclined to do—that there are correct and incorrect versions of oral rhymes, the lore will begin to become rigid, and eventually it will die. Then the cultured will be correct when they think English cities have no sub-cultures of their own.

I

CHARGE OF THE SCOUSE BRIGADE

SHALL I BEGIN IT?

> Arf a leg, arf a leg, arf a leg of mutton
> Into the pan a scouse rolled the six onions.

Cheer Up the Scotty Lads

Cheer up the Scotty Lads, you're winning everywhere,
You knocked the dirty Kirkdale lads, Flyin' in the air,
If they ask for mercy—Mercy won't be there,
Cheer up the Scotty lads, you're winning everywhere.

The Shinback Fusileers

> Eyes right, Shinbacks tight,
> Scotty to the rear,
> We're the boys that fear no noise—
> And we're always on the beer.
> We're the heroes of the night,
> And we'd rather run than fight,
> We're the heroes of the Shinback Fusileers.

Taught by elders, *c*. 1915.

'Shinback', 'run' are euphemisms. Used in street wars which were not as fierce as the rattling of dustbin lids suggested. These were shields. Weapons, bricks, old cans, wooden swords. Marching songs, often parodies, in the line of Slattery's Mounted Foot and The Ballyhooley Blue Ribbon Army, feature of Liverpool life, even adult.

Tramp Tramp

Tramp, tramp, tramp, the boys are marchin'
Eh, up, the bobby's at the dooor—
    If you don't let him in
    He will burst the door in,
And you'll never see yer mammy any more.

c. 1915.

Before Decimals

Rule Britannia,
Two tanners make a bob,
Three make eighteen pence,
And four make two bob.

Left, Right

I had a good job and I
    Left Right.

Three Cheers for the Red, White and Blue

Three cheers for the red, white and blue,
It sticks to yer belly like glue.
        or
    Are you workin'?
    No, are you?
Then three cheers for, etc.

Papist Marching Song

King Billy's mother
Keeps a hoor-ouze in ell . . .

Our Sol

Our soldiers went to war,
With pistols in their hands,
For curiosity
I'll fight for my ol'—
    I'll fight for my ol'—
I'll fight for me old countree.

Throughout the compiler feels he must tread a tightrope between authenticity and decency.

Our soldiers went to war.
Our soldiers won.
Our soldiers stuck a bay-nit up the Kayser's
Our sol—.

Proddy Dog Barks Back

Ee, ay, Paddy, was a bastid,
Paddy was a bastid—EEE, ay, oh . . .

The Free Churches never marched!

We Are the English Soldiers

A 70-year old Scouser gave me this first line which he used marching to school, in 1960, but he gave me no more.— DISMISS! FORWARD MAARCH!

To ARMS and a wooden leg—
March on, march on . . .

THE SCHOOL BELL
or 'Your Penny a Week Wuz Wastid'

You're late, you're late,
The bobby's at the gate.

Chimbley's on Fire

Chimbley's on fire,
The bobby's a liar.

As I write, there is concern over children, owing to the winterisation of Summer Time, going to school in darkness. We went, years ago, if not through factory smoke, when smokeless zones were unheard of, through the effluent of chimneys set afire early on to avoid paying the sweep's fee of sixpence or so.

Skip Over the Cobbles, Kids!

One, two, three, Mother cot a flea,
She put it in the teapot, An' made a cup of tea.
The flea jumped out, me mother give a shout an'
Up comes the bobby wit his shirt hanging out.

No doubt about it, bobbies and shirts are funny.

'Present, Miss!'

And I keep singing in my heart,
Don't mark me late,
Don't mark me late.

R.C. children's parody on the lovely May hymn to the Virgin, Immaculate, Immaculate. This sort of simple irreverence is no more culpable than the version of 'Pray for us' I've heard from farm labourers in Ireland, kneeling on a stony kitchen floor when, after a long Rosary, a long Litany was embarked on by the Man of the House—'Make tay for us, make tay for us.' Such kids read AMDG (Ad Maiorem Dei Gloriam) on top of the hymn card as All Mad Donkeys Gallop and LDS (Laus Deo Semper) on the bottom. Last Down Stinks. A R.C. headmaster reminds me IHS on altar cloth (Iesus Hominum Salvator) was I Have Suffered and backwards, So Have I.

Morning Prayer

Me Mother and Father was Irish
And I was Irish too,
We bought a old kettle for ninepence—*
And dat was Irish too.*

What'll we do if the kettle boils over ?
What'll we do But sell it again.

What'll she do if she goes for a sodger ?
What'll she do but marry again.

*Or 'We kept an old pig in the parlour'.

Ifff—me father an' me mother Adden missed
the boat for I-er-land I might   (*fortissimo*)
ave been a Ir-ish-man.

NOTES

(i) 'Your penny a week was wasted' is nearly a century old, going back to the beginnings of education for the majority. Nothing for nowt in those days and in my youth it was quite usual to hear old people refer to the penny a week once paid for national elementary education. There were small charges even in my time. Big ones at the 'secondary' school. The old terms stick whatever new names are given to the strata right up to 'incomprehensive.' Standards, forms, Monitors, prefects, Drill, P.T.

New presybter is only priest writ large as workhouses are still workhouses and midden-men sanitary officers.

(ii) 'The bobby's at the gate' is even older. In a fifteenth-century rhyme we find 'The times are waxing late, The judge is at the gate.' *Hymns A. & M.* has 'The world is very evil, The times are waxing late, Be sober and keep vigil The Judge is at the gate.' (J. N. Neale, transl. from Bernard of Miles.)

(iii) If, bobby lying or not, one was arrested for Chimbley on fire it could be a domestic tragedy. Cases were treated on an assembly line, five bob fine, five bob costs. A week's house-keeping money sixty years ago. A backstreet lawyer who pleaded Not Guilty, said, 'I didn't do it deliberately.' To which the Stipendiary mildly replied, 'I sincerely hope not. Otherwise you would be here on the more serious charge of arson. Ten shillings and ten shillings.'

Roll Call

What's yer name?
> Mary Jane.

Where d'you live?
> Down the grid.

What number?
> Cucumber.

What house?
> Pig scouse.

It was 'butter and crame' in my Irish kindergarten before I came to Liverpool. At that the rhyme is no worse than live—grid. But see page 131 for rhymes generally.

School Song

S-F-X, S-F-X, Saint Francis Xavier's,*
School for the Northerner, School for the Southerner,
Easterner, Westerner, Layman or Cleric,
A school that is truly grand—
Saint Francis Xavier's.

*The X is seldom silent.

Talk about rhymes! I sang it over fifty years ago and, to me, it is, no I'm a liar, like The Eton Boating Song or Forty Years On. Author, Anon, a teacher no doubt. No worse than any other school song. Or most national anthems.

Pre-History

In days of old, When knights were bold
And paper had not been invented,
They wiped theirselfs On telegraph poles
And—Walked away contented.

1915. I heard, on a farm where Liverpool schoolboys were holidaying while working. Rhyming to different words for theirselfs, an alternative in the third line to telegraph poles was broken glass, selfs itself having replaced a rhyming word. . . .

Farming Intelligence

I can see her now Down at Farmer Fenn's
Picking up the newlaid eggs from the cow
And milking the cocks and hens.
                              —Late Victorian.

'Come Out That Boy!'

Ow!
Say soap!—A tug at the rope.
                    —He had pulled her pigtail.

Miss F...

Miss F
          Miss A   Miss Z A K
                   Miss E   Miss R
Miss L   E   Y

                                        c. 1906.

Taught to children in Fazakerley, a Liverpool suburb, to teach them how to pronounce its difficult name, based on that of an old Lancashire family. The kids of Cabbage Hall and Knotty Ash and Copperas Hill got by.

Multiplication

Twice one are two, Twice two are four,
Twice three are six,
          And there's kids on the floor.

In Nineteen Hundred and Ten
The Women Ran After the Men

Once upon a time, When the birds made lime,
          And monkeys chewed t'backo
The old women come, With their fingers on their bum
          To see what was the matter.
The matter was the bricklayers had no mortar.
Up come a little bird, And he made a little turd,
          And the bricklayers had some mortar.

If I have felt, as occasionally elsewhere, I must let Dr.

Bowdler in—you still have tittering Nurse Imagination. The cameo is still a delightful one.

Heard on that farm fifty years ago.

Sixth Standard Chemistry

> Pour ould Billy Nitt
> > The man that is no more.
> > What he took for H_2O was H_2SO_4.

And he might, like the girl in the Liverpool group, The Scaffolds', song, 'Lily the Pink', have discovered 'a medicinal compound' and been a 'saviour of the human race'.

Spelling

> If an S and an I and an O and a U with an X at the end
> spells Sioux,
> > And an E and a Y and an E spells eye—
> Pray what is a speller to do?
> > If an S and an I and a G and an H and an E and a D
> spells sighed,
> > Pray what is there left for a speller to do but—
> To go and commit Sioux-eye-sighed?

This, given to me in 1920 by an elderly butcher, taught in St. Nicholas School, Liverpool, by an Irish teacher in the last century, was, he said, chanted by the boys, though obviously it had a written origin.

He also had 'Multiplication is my vexation'—at an 'elementary' school. Quoted in *Forget-me-Not Annual* for 1846!

'Can I Leave the Room, Please?'

> Miss, Miss, I wanna kiss.
> Or a ruder rhyme, according to how deaf Miss is.
> See North Walian Emlyn Williams's *The Corn is Green*.

And have I not heard
> 'Miss, Miss, Jimmy Green's
> Left the room on the floor!'

Saint Columba's, 1944. Playtime

> We are the Huyton lads,
> Happy as can be,
> Teachers say we're hardfaced,*
> Then hardfaced we will be.
> (Waiting for the school bell
> SO WE CAN BE FREE)

> If it wasn't for the Huyton lads
> Where would the teachers be?
> On the dole—on the dole—
> We'd like to see the teachers on the dole.

*cheeky

Recalled, with others herein, by Michael Francis Xavier Shaw, B.A.

Music Lesson

> Do re me fa so la te do
> O, please don't stand on my big toe.

For the four spaces FACE was easy enough to recall but EGBDF became
> Eat Good Bread Dear Father

More Music

> (*Up*) Doh ray me fah soh lah te doh
> I've lost me knickers in the snow.
> (*Down*) If you find 'em please let me know
> Doh te lah soh fah me ray doh.

This came, per Meirion Roberts, from Llanwyrst to Liverpool, like so many of its natives, from the Land of Song.

French Lesson

Parlee vooze Fransie madam-mer-selle
Went to the lavatory and in she fell—
When she come back, oh, what a smell
Parlee vooze Fransie madam-mer-selle.

After many years Mrs. Morris now of Coventry wonders why the French teacher objected to this. Mrs. M. was 5. 'My father was delighted with it!' Froggies!

But what about this recalled more than 60 years after by Mrs. A. E. Stott now in Sheffield? 'She overheard it in the schoolyard and caned us all up and down it.'

O have you been to France?
To see Miss Siderkin dance?
She kicked her leg up high
And showed her apple pie.

Music from *Orpheus in the Underworld*.

Our Teacher

Doctor Foster's a very good man
He teaches children all he can,
Reading, writing, arithmetic
And never forgets to use his stick.
Out of England, into France,
Out of France and into Spain,
Over the sea and back again.

Mrs. Scott of Liverpool 25, one of the many locally and

from far afield recalling this for more than half a century (the name Foster fairly persistent) with

> Mister Chips is a very good man
> He goes to church on Sunday,
> To pray to God To give him strength
> To larrup the lads on Monday.

Four teachers recalled after 30 years:

> Miss Lamb caught a lamb,
> Miss Skinner skinned it,
> Miss Cross crossed its legs,
> Mr. Duff ate* it.

*To rhyme with *plate*.

Geography

(i)

> England, Ireland, Scotland, Wales,
> All put together make a fine pair of scales.

(ii)

> Austria was Hungary, stole a bit of Turkey,
> dipped in Greece and Italy
> Kicked poor Sicily
> Into the Medi-terranean Sea.

(iii)

> Constantinople's a very fine word. Spell it.

I T, it. Get it? Then keep it. See the point? Well, sit on it. How many wells make a river? Two and your head makes it bigger.

The Constantinople item, which probably started, like FAZAKERLEY, as a teacher's mnemonic—a pedagogic device as old as the hills—became part of a popular song like the kids' Mairsy doats and doazy doats An' little lambsy tivy (Mares eat oats and does eat oats and little lambs eat ivy) which Tommy Handley rendered as Mersey Docks and Harbour Board.

Latin for Beginners

Amo, amas, I loved a lass,
My love for her was tender;
Alas, alack, she fell down flat
Upon her feminine gender.

Different version in *B.O.P.* 1890, I am told.

Roman History

She wants you to do as the Romans do—
Oh, Julius cease—'er.

Popular song, *c.* 1920.

Julius Ceasar let a beezer
Off the coast of France,
Hitler tried to do the same, and did it in his pants.

A Liverpool fried fish shop proprietor during the terrible 1941 blitz had a notice put in his window:

'Thanks to Hitler
Our portions are littler.'

Anything like that suited the school-less kids who took it up readily. But I cannot prove that one depraved damsel did not add:

'Thanks to Go-ring I've gone back to Rhuddlan'

(Welsh home of first 'vaccies'). A Liverpool kid during hours in a shelter, sitting in the dark, gave us an unconscious rhyme:

'Eh, mum, Me bum's num.'

Breaking Up

Teacher's rest, Mother's pest,
Father's on the dole.

c. 1922.

Mothers weren't too fond of teachers either. After all, usually from the same class and not by mum's standards underpaid. Certainly they were over-holidayed. So mid-term break to mams with unemployed adults in the house was just a nuisance; teachers—whose holidays are too long after all, hated the rhyme.

On the term's last day, Kid One to Kid Two: 'Have you brought yer hammer?'

Two: 'No, why?'

One: ''Cos we're breaking up today.'

Posh schools, of course, had the rhyme about No more Latin, no more French, which is at least a century old.

Teachers were indeed forty years ago snooty and often sadistic but smarter in appearance, apparently better conducted and certainly better instructors than the current crop.

Deo Gratias

My humble thanks I'll now return,
My soul is filled with joy.—
I'm at the Kirkdale Ragged Home—
But not a homeless boy.

Liverpool school song, c. 1900, quoted in *A Great Life, The Life of Major Lester*, anon, 1909. Major (Christian name, not title) Lester of whom, with Fr. Nugent, a similar Catholic priest philanthropist—he was Anglican—of the last century, there is a statue in the city's central St. John's Gardens (a former burial-ground) with a set piece of the Boer War and stone replicas of political forgottens bearing the words, as he holds a barefooted lad: Give the boy a chance. He founded 'ragged' schools—no euphemisms amongst social reformers then.

Mystery Carol

Fifty years ago before the Christmas holidays Liverpool schoolchildren sang this carol. No modern 'Pool kids know it.

But, when Glyn Hughes asks pensioners at their clubs when he goes to play banjo to them, all the old girls and boys know it. With so much remembered how was this forgotten?

> The snow fell fast in December
> The wintry winds did roar
> When a poor young raggedy sailor boy
> Came passing a lady's door.
>
> The lady looked out of the window
> And opened the parlour door:
> 'Come in, me poor young sailor boy,
> And go to sea no more.'
>
> 'I once had a sailor boy lost at sea
> He was my pride and joy,
> As long as I live, A shelter I'll give
> To a poor young sailor boy.'

We-elll! A former resident in Knotty Ash writing to the *Prescot and Huyton Reporter* from Toronto early in 1969 created a correspondence which made it clear that in the mid-forties boys from that Liverpool district—oh, yes, it exists all right and I once lived there near Squire Dodd!—knew this carol well and sang it. I have since, thanks to Head Miriam Sadowski, heard the junior boys at Knotty Ash School myself.

III

FRIENDS AND NEIGHBOURS

You know me Anty Nellie,
She had a wooden belly,
*   An' ev'ry time you knock her down—*
Three shies a penny.

Nelly's Sister Anna

Nelly's sister Anna wanted to buy a piano
But her father said 'No,
I'll buy you a po
And then you can have a pee-Anna.'

Mrs. Reeve sending me this from Stoke-on-Trent added 'not too old to enjoy a laugh'.

The Irish Exhibitionist

Paddy went walkin' one fine day
    He lost his breeches on the way,
The men did laff, The women did stare
To see poor Paddy with his bum all bare.

Old King Cole

Old King Cole was a merry old soul.
A merry old soul was he,
He called for a light

In the middle of the night
To go the the W.C.

One of the many versions, the cleanest.

Our Sally's New Drawers

Our Sally's new drawers,
Our Sally's new drawers,
There's a hole in the middle
For Sally to piddle
In our Sally's new drawers.

May Wiggins of Bolton one of many who recalled.

When the compiler wrote an essay on Liverpool street rhymes for Liverpool University's very permissive mag. *Sphinx*, the very avant-garde editorial staff hesitated to print this which old ladies at a Huyton W.R.V.S. tea-and-cake do had chanted gaily and without self-consciousness, with Nelly's Sister Anna and many another relic of playground ribaldry for the writer.

Little Dolly Daydream

Little Dolly Daydream went to ride a bike
She tumbled off
It made her cough
And all the buttons on her bloomers come off.

Me Uncil Joe

Me Uncil Joe
          He was a savidge,
He dipped his nose
          In pickled cabbidge,

He ate the meat,
     An' chewed the gristle an'
That is how he learnt to
     Whistle.

Paddy Irish

Paddy Irish sells fish, Three ha'pence a dish,
If you don't like Paddy Irish
     You won't like his fish.

Cp. Johnson 'If a man who turnips cries' for non sequitur.

Some children sang, for 'Paddy Irish,' 'Sally Army' or 'Daddy Bunchy.'

Billy the Barber

Billy the Barber shaved his father,
Wid a rusty razor.
     The razor slipped
     An' cut his lip—
*Hurray for Billy the Barber.

*Or 'alas'. This wouldn't be the Everton barber whose slogan became a kids' street chant: Leave yer hair to Jackson's care?

Bill Moore's gloss for 'Billy' 'Sally Army' has no provenance.

Eddie Jones

Eddie Jones broke his bones
     Tumblin' over cherrystones.

P.C. Knockabout

P.C. Knockabout wagged his cockabout
Behind the fac-try wall,
It made such a rattle
It sounded like a battle
Beyond the fac'try wall.

Hippy Clergy

There were two Irish priests
Who sang upon the altar,
When they went out
The kids would shout
ARCHIBALD AND WALTER.

How did that one get to Manchester, Mrs. Morgan?

Me Father Was a Navvy

Me father was a navvy
Working on the line
Earning twenty-four and six
Besides his overtime;
He gives his tart a guinca,
A golden ring beside
And then she has the cheek to ask him
To take her for a ride.

I Wish I Was a Bobby

I wish I was a bobby
Dressed in bobby's clothes,

A big tall hat
A belly full of fat
And a pancake stuck to me nose.

Since Bobby Peel's day the Bobby, the Peeler, from top hat to helmet to cap, has always been associated with food, so in kids' comic, twenties, P.C. Cuddlecook.—Ta, John Atkinson.

Strange Sort of Chap, Would You Say?

Charlie, Charlie, chuch, chuck, chuck,
Went to bed with three lame ducks.

I Don't Want None of Yer Stinkin' Fish

I don't want none of yer blarney,
I don't want none of yer stinkin' fish,
Away and jine the Army.

Bill Cogley, former Liverpool headmaster, who gave me much herein, had for 'blarney' 'garnet'. Back street money lenders gave some of the loan in stinking fish. I know. We lived next door to one. Last line:

Oh dirty Mrs. McGarney.

Who was she?

Owen More

Owen More went away.
Owen more than he could pay.
Owen More
Come back again.—Owen More.

—1913.

Show me Sally sitting in her china shop.—There were many

tongue twisters tempting the correct into unwonted impropriety.

Johnny

Johnny in his football jersey
Fell into the River Mersey.
'Ring me up from Birkenhead
When yer get there' his old man said.

Would this, sung about 1912 by boys on a camp holiday in North Wales from Liverpool, later in print in a church magazine (written, I think, by Frank Radcliffe, S.J.) be the first ruthless rhyme? Before Harry Graham?

Another

The boy stood on the tramlines,
The driver rang the bell.—
The tram went on to Anfield
The little boy went to ——well—

The curious timidity, reminding one of Frank Harris's unexpected use of d——l, doesn't match the harmlessly naughty use of more verboten words out of parental/teacher hearing. I first heard 1919.

Jackie Gordon

Oo-ey, Jackie Gordon, are you coming out?

Not necessarily to Jackie Gordon of course, though a teacher who has helped me with this book gave me her recollection of calling this through the letter box of his home to this boy, God rest his soul.

It fits what the other Shaw said about Woman the Chaser,

but not the next rhyme which Liverpool singers, teachers too,
Jacqueline and Bridie, have so nicely set to their guitars.

I'll Tell Ma

I'll tell Ma
When she gets home,
The boys won't leave the girls alone.

Mary Ann Shee

Mary Ann she,
Locked the door and turned the key.

Probably like Queenie, Queenie counting rhyme, but our
informant couldn't recall.

From a teenager; all informants were not greybeards.

Jeremiah

Jeremiah pee'd on the fire.
The fire was out—
So he pee'd up the spout.
The spout was flat
So he pee'd on the cat
And the cat ran away
With the pee on its back.

Little Willy Wheelbarrow

Little Willy Wheelbarrow wheels a barrow genter-lee
Don't make a noise, Get the middens empter-lee—
Twelve o'clock at night running through the enter-ee
With a barrow full of—

Sweet Vi-or-lets—
Wheel the barrow gently.

—Not so long ago.

Old Jacobite Rhyme?

Charlie over the water,
Charlie over the sea,
Charlie wet his breeches—
And put the blame on me?

Or would Charlie have had 'breeches'? I remember being taken home by a big boy after a worse disaster and his four-letter description of it!

He's a nice little feller
But his legs are yeller.

This, *c.* 1912, has a vague excremental association like the alleged Chinese laundryman's 'Nicoteeney on shirtee tuppence extla'.

When Dixie Dean
Was seventeen
He tried to score a goal.
He missed his chance
And ripped his pants
And now he's on the dole.

Lovely to think of a little girl on the Lollipop Man's crossing in Rossy (Roscommon Street) singing this nearly half a century after the great footballer, who incidentally hated that, Dixie was seventeen and starting a career in which he missed few goals as centre for Everton and eventually beat the record for most goals in first-class professional soccer.

Taffy Jones

Taffy Jones is a fool
Tied his stockings to a stool.
When the stool began to crack
All the bugs run up his back.

Lads knew more about Keatings than about Keats in the days of bug-ridden furniture.

Bessie

I know a fat girl
Twice as fat as me
She had muscles on her arms like the branches of a tree;
She can run, jump, skip,
Anything at all
She can jump over jiggers and up a back wall.

Liverpool lads, and girls, are still intrepid climbers though the back lanes, or jiggers, with the walls of overbuilt houses on each side up which, with little purchase, barefooted, one foot each side, they could climb on to a roof and run along it like a cat, are dying. The Scouser into middle years will never go a few yards walk if a jump over or climb up a wall will save him a minute, as can be seen daily in the new suburbs.

The sender of that who lives in Binns Road, Liverpool, where Meccano and Hornby Trains come from also, recalled others which 'originated in the Kings Liverpool Regiment' and that should explain why the Washerwoman starting 'full of hope' fell on such a tender spot when she tripped on 'carbolic soap.'

Hello, Mrs. Tuckett,
I found yer bucket
And I know who took it.

Sister Mary

Sister Mary, walks like that,
    pit a pat, pit a pat.

Mimicry followed. Maybe of Sister of Mercy, in quondam habit.

Queenie, Queenie

Queenie, Queenie, Who's got the ball?
I haven't got it. It isn't in my pocket.
Queenie, Queenie, Who's got the ball?

Holy Joe

Holy Joe the minister,
    Dipped his nose in
Vinegar.

Nitty Nora

Nitty Nora
'Sback in town.

c. 1940.

Daddy Bunchy (i)

Daddy Bunchy the dirty ould man,
Washes his socks in the likkle egg-pan,
Dries his kecks*
    In the fryin pan.

*Trousers.
We had many versions of Dan, Dan, the dirty old man

(South Country 'lavatory man') which all go back of course to King George IV's Queen Caroline, allegedly a slut who combed her hair with the leg of a chair, etc.

Daddy Bunchy (ii)

Up the steps, up the steps,
. . . to Daddy Bunchy park.

The steps were steep in Everton, to the park almost on the spot of the first Everton Toffee Shop and the nearest invading Prince Rupert got to Liverpool.

But who was Daddy Bunchy, who knows? Glyn doesn't after careful inquiry and discarding with me, idea that he was a 'bogey.' Might as well ask who Joe Gerk, Dick Tutt or Hicky the Firebobby were. Figures, like Lob Lie by the Fire, in our urban mythology.

Rhyme probably came from counting game. At least sixty years old. False antiquarians also have him robbing Paddy Irish of his fish trade, almost once an Irish monopoly.

Mary Ellen

Mary Ellen, Mary Ellen, Mary Ellen, does yer mother know yer out?

Mary Ellen, Mary Ellen, Mary Ellen, As she goes down Scotty Road you'll hear them shout,

Mary Ellen, Mary Ellen, Mary Ellen, Mary Ellen, does yer mother know yer out?

c. 1910.

Mary (actually sounded as Murry as in the R.C. hymn Daily, Daily, sing to Murry) Ellen has come to mean a rough 'bucko' girl, a shawlie, a market woman of the kind whose chant the kids used to imitate—alas, like our barrer boys, a dying race. This 'ere progress, it keeps going on—unfortunately.

> 'Sage a mint a parsley—Buy a bag, lady?
> Apples a pound, pears. Grapes we 'ave none,
> Buy me last one an' I'll give yer six.—
> Say anudder word and I'll 'it yer wit the scales—
> Sage a mint a parsley.'

To his chant a barrow boy added in true Scouse extempore mode:

> Israel oranges, Very Jewsy.

Belly Laff

> Mrs. Jones, bag of bones,
> Sailing down the river.
> A fish come up and bit her bum
> And made her belly shiver.

Ta, Mrs. Burgess.

It's That Man Again

> By the cross, by the cross
> Where the Kaiser lost his hoss
> And the Eagle from his hat blew away.
> He was eating Berlin buns
> When he heard the British guns
> And the nasty little beggar ran away.

Johnny Todd

> Johnny Todd he took a notion
> For to cross the raging sea,
> And he left his true love behind him,

Weeping by the Liverpool sea.
　　　For a week she wept full sorely,
Tore her hair and wrung her hands
Till she met with another sailor
Walking on the Liverpool sands.

He promises her 'all sorts', including a pram, even a ring, so when Johnny came home 'over the ocean wide' he found:

His fair and false one
Was another sailor's bride.
　　　　So
All young men who go a-sailing
For to fight the foreign foe,
Don't you leave your love like Johnny,
Marry her before you go.
　　　　　　First collected by Kidson in 1891.

(Just before that date a Johnny Todd was actually hanged in a Liverpool gaol.) It was a skipping game used by Liverpool children, as said the Liverpool musician who with wife turned it into the memorable 'Z Cars Theme' (arranged by Fritz Spiegl and Bridget Fry). Sung by Ewan McColl, Liverpool's Stan Kelly in Denis Mitchell's Liverpool documentary, *Morning in the Streets*, and, 1969, Glyn Hughes for Denis Mitchell's Liverpool documentary featuring Frank Shaw, it has become a sort of Scouseport anthem, more authentically Scouse than 'Maggie May'—which kids don't sing—and the tune is played weekly at Everton football games. . . .

The *Daily Mirror* reported in 1968, 7th October, a New Forest choir were using tune for hymn 'Father Hear Our Prayers', as Liverpool Orange Ladies once used it for their 'hymns.' . . .

The Ould Feller

Never light the fire wid yer father's wooden leg,
Never strike a match on yer ould feller's baldy patch . . .

Don't throw stones at yer father——
>Throw bricks at yer mother in-stead.

Dominic Behan recalls much the same lyric in Dublin. But
—who gave what to which? As in next:

>Ould woman, ould woman I hate yer,
>>I'll get a big sthick and I'll bate yer.

How many poor old girls in city backstreets, living alone,
regarded as Old Witches for no reason, did we bait with this?
But, all is well,

>>For the angels above Sent a pint in a jug,
>>To that old fashioned mother o' mine.

Patsy Finegan

>Let your nannan* grow
>Let yer whiskers blow,
>Why waste money on shav-avin'?
>Pull 'em out be the roots,
>Make laces for yer boots,
>Look at the money yer sa-avin'.

We brought Patsy into our assembly of mythical figures like
Paddy Irish and Hicky the Firebobby: he's the man in the
song who grew whiskers on his chinegan and the wind came
out and blew them in agen and, later, in our own verse, grew
his own tobacco on his chest.
*Beard.

K-K-K-K-Katie

>K-K-K-K-Katie
>She swallered a ha'peny,
>She's the only g-g-g-g-g-girl that I adore.

  The night before dat
  She swallered a doormat, Now
We're looking for the k-k-k-k-k-key of the kitchen door.

From a twenties song still, they tell me, used as a ball-bouncing rhyme.

Our Bob

  Our Bob, owes your Bob A bob*.
   Our Bob says that if your Bob
  doesn't give our Bob The bob
  That your Bob owes our Bob, Our Bob
  Will give your Bob
   A bob in the eye.

*Shilling, punch. Cp. 'Conny Onny' and 'Where You Goin' Joe?'

There's a Bobby Down Our Street

  Now I'm an ould copper and I knows me book,
  I can tell 'em wid a saucy look.
  —Round I go to people's houses,
  Dust the seats of youngster's trousers . . .

Recalled from *c.* 1900 and obviously from music-hall song though shouted after the local slop.
  So Eck, eck, pick the ball up, fellers.

Liverpool Boys

  LIVERPOOL BOYS are merry, merry boys
  BIRKENHEAD BOYS ARE BETTER
    (*all together, girls*)
  If I ketch a Birkenhead boy I'll—
  Give him a dose of pepper.

Daddy Chrismus

Daddy Chrismus, guess what he did?
Upset the cradle and out fell the kid.
The kid began to bubble
He hit it with the shovel,
Little Daddy Chrismus
That's what he did.

In our big shop fairs or 'grottos' ('Don't open your parcel
till you get home') we had some rare ould Daddy Christmases
—One arrived by helicopter on the shop roof and was sick all
over the first kid he kissed; another was 'dipping' mam's
handbag as he kissed the nipper. What value the kid got besides
his tanner parcel—real fairies rather overblown from the
haberdashery department, real sand, a mechanical piano, a
wonderland until—*disillusion:*

I've seen Santa Claus
Me and me little brother—
He brings the toys
For girls and boys
And gets in bed with mother.

NOTES
(i) *Daddy Bunchy.* This mysterious man crops up in a
children's skipping game more than 60 years old according to
Miss Wooley of Southport who sent me other games included,
in a few instances (as some are already well-known and in
print) in Chapter VI. (It was lovely to meet again 'There was
a man, a man indeed Sewed a garden full of seed,' my mother's
favourite but not really a children's rhyme in my sense.)
In Miss Wooley's a big girl, as mother, puts her apron over
her head like a tent (Apron!) and chants:
'Who goes round my store house tonight?'
Daddy Bunchy. 'Bunchy, Bunchy, only Daddy Bunchy.'

Mother. 'Don't take away any of my fine chickens.'

D.B. 'Only, only—this fine one.' (Kids are kneeling round.)

D.B. 'This fine one.' He snatches one of kids, who leaves ring and goes behind the lad playing D.B. and puts her hand on his shoulder, so till all the kids behind him. Mother dodges round trying to catch them. Chase. Last one caught is new D.B. Now how did he get to urban Liverpool? And our park?

Miss Wooley, by the way, recalled the sensation the first women bikeriders in 'bloomers' caused in a Liverpool street!

(ii) *Dan, Dan*. And, lo he leads the rest. I thought to leave him out but readers assure me we can no more have a collection of kids' rhymes without 'Dan, Dan (or Sam, Sam) the dirty old man' than 'Charlie Chaplin' upon whom the 'sun shone bright'. In the summer of 1969 as a result of Press and radio publicity in the North of England (see final section of book, 'Instead of a Preface') I received from readers evidence that he was the most recalled from childhood by my ageing readers though in varying forms and with differing degrees of rudery. As he became Daddy Bunchy he was mixed with the 'Taffy' who was 'a thief' who, another injustice to ould Ireland, himself became Paddy. But he always combed his hair with the leg of a chair and used his big toenail.

In apologising for almost leaving him out I note, with a sniff, a variant:

> Picking out the finals
> From all of the urinals.

The coyness of the spinster Miss of years ago towards the natural needs of kids inured to communal 'closets', Dad's unconcealed use of chamber-pot, old girls outside pubs standing in their long dresses over grids to urinate, led to the cloacal emphasis in many of the kids' private rhymes. They half hoped the prim pedagogue would overhear and be shocked by their 'cacky' expressions. When the dancing boy or wriggling girl, waving a hand with growing anxiety, finally caught her eye and she heard their request she might add 'Number One or Number Two?' To the sons and daughters of Liverpool dockers and ship's firemen!

(iii) *Holy Joe the Minister* did more than dip his nose in vinegar. In this collection I often know of course more of a rhyme than I give. But I never knew the rest of the Holy Joe saga,

> When the vinegar began to start he made a rude noise.
> When the 'noise' began to stop
> Holy Joe began to cough.
> Holy Joe began to sneeze
> With his head between his knees,
> Holy Joe looked up and sighed,
> Holy Joe lay down and died.

Ta Mr. Stoddard.

(iv) *Variant of Anty Nelly* surprised me:

> You know me Uncle Jack?
> He had a wooden back,
> Every time you knocked him down
> You got your money back.

IV

FOOD AND DRINK

Who likes gravy on his taters,
Who likes taters in his tin?
Taters in a tin.
Enough to make you grin.
Who likes gravy on his taters?

All In

All in
        a bokkle of gin
All out
        a bokkle of stout.

The Rabbit Pie

The rabbit pie it sat upon the able,
We all made a rush for the door.
My Old Man—He fainted on the chair,
And I fell through the floor.

(Bish, bang)

The cat started laughing, the dog dropped dead,
The monkey up the chimbley done a guy.*
As long as I live, I'll never forget—
The night-we-had-the-rabbit-pie.

*'Done a guy', departed hurriedly.

About 1912. An authentic pre-myxomatosis domestic interior which is still touching.

They Don't Even Taste the Same

A penn'orth a chips, An' a a'port a peas—
An' after you Wit the vineger please.

c. 1914.

Down Memory Lane

Follow your mother to the treacle shop, treacle shop
Follow your mother to the treacle shop—
And where d'you think I found her?
In the lobby Kissing a bobby
And the kids all around her.

Ta for reminding me, Mrs. Hoyle and do you recall, as Mrs. Pownall of Wallasey does, the Treacle Cart from which you could buy the stuff twopence a pint, licking the overspill off your fingers on your way from cart to kitchen? She also recalls the Salt Man and the many other street callers the modern kids know not, and it's their loss.

Rosie made a pudden
She made it very sweet,
But dare not stick her fork home
Till Dad come home to eat;
Daddy will you have a bit, don't say no,
For on Monday morning to a wedding we'll go.

Cheese It!

(i)
Me Mother bought some cheese
She made me Father sneeze,

The cat had a fit in the cellar,
The dog had a heart disease—
The chair began to walk,
The table did the same,
And me granmother's—luvly—picture—
Fell out of its gol-den frame.

Came down the Manchester Ship Canal from Mrs. Roome in Swinton.

(ii)
I bought a pennorth of mouldy cheese
And I put it behind the door;
When I got up next morning
It was dancing across the floor—
Singing Yankee Doodle, Yankee Doodle,
I'm the Cock o' the North.

Go to sleep before you have your dinner.
Never had a dinner in my life.
Here I am, very fond of kippers.
Never had a kipper in me life.

70 years old at least.

Finish It Yourself—It's Too Hot For Me

Colman's mustard, Colman's starch—Tell Mr. Colman to ——

A Welsh girl again, Mrs. Goodwin from Aberystwyth.

Afters

Apple pie is very nice
So is apple pasty.
Johnny Smith wet the bed
And that was *very nasty*.

A Little Poem Entitled—

The saveloy flew into a passion
And handed the sausage his card,
And offered to fight in a duel
In my old feller's backyard;
The sausage accepted the challenge
You're a coward, he cries,
To strike down a likkle sausage,
Only a quarter your size.
The sausage trembled at the knees
And asked for pen and paper please
To tell his mother how he dies.
I knew his mother well, sir,
For years they played together, sausage and saveloy,
Sharing each other's troubles
Sharing each other's joy—
Have they to part like this, Bill?
So cried a piece of steak—
Shake hands and let us be friends
               For old time sake.

c. 1913

OXO (A Square Meal)

As the kids walk down the street
They advertise extract of meat.
          (*They shape the letters*)
The middle one he made the word, OXO
You cannot miss,
For a bow-legged boy walked on each side
And the middle one walked like this O.

'I've sung this catchy tune for 60 years' John Cocker tells
me.

Nelly

Nelly ate some pastry, Nelly ate some jelly
Nelly went to bed wit
                    A pain in her
Don't be mistaken, don't be misled,
Nelly went to bed with
                    A pain in her head.

Caught yer, eh?

            The boy stood on the burning deck
            A leg of mutton round his neck.

Is the famous poem by Liverpool's Felicia Hemans, the
most parodied poem in the language? We kids knew many
other versions.

Send Him Victorious

Send him victorious,
            Half a pound of meat among four of us,
Not enough for two of us,
                    God Save——

In the hungry Twenties. Good days or bad, Liverpool kids
and their dads excel in parody.

A'Penny Cornet Mister
('I scream for ice cream')

Okey pokey, penny a lump,
Just the thing to make you jump.

A Manchester reader prefers 'Just come out of the horse's
rump.'

Nobody in the world to equal Liverpool's ice cream merchants of yesteryear.

Conny Onny

*Conny onny, naughty Tommie
Eating Noblett's Toffee Sticks.

*Conny onny, condensed milk.

A Liverpool singer, Sheila Donnahey, recalls how, on bread, for God's sake, we loved it as kids, in a fine song. (Well, she sang it with Glyn and me in OUR show!) The initial letters of the rhyme spell out CONTENTS as seen in the school books. For other version see Chapter V. Noblett's toffee is the toffee which made Everton famous. Mother Noblett is the lady in Cranford costume, well-known on shop-fronts and hoardings to an earlier generation, who still represents Everton football team (The Toffees) in cartoons; a girl dressed this way runs round the ground before games, with gamp. Actually Mother Noblett did not invent the toffee, which Dickens during his many visits to the port used to buy for his sons, but a Maggie Bushell. And she had the still-not-revealed recipe from an Everton doctor—who made it as a medicine. Take that, you Everton F.C. supporters. Dickens lodged with a Mr. Shaw near the old toffee-shop, in Breck Road, Everton (now town-planned out of existence with so very much more of the old midden) and there one day he had lunch with a Miss Weller. He had met her the night before at a 'swarry' in the Mechanics' Institute where she was playing piano. She later married Dickens' friend T. J. Thompson and had two daughters who gained fame, Lady Butler painter of 'Balaclava' and Alice Meynell. *The Dickensian* for January 1916 had long piece about the pianist Christina Weller. In a letter to her sister C.D., who knew our city well, especially the dockside slums (he was a special constable in the port's force!) said Liverpudlians were 'the most considerate people in the world.' (And is that my longest footnote? Wait for it!)

Pork and Beans

Pork and beans is a Yankee dish
But give me Sunday mornin' an' the ould salt fish.

We learnt it from our dads, many familiar with the New
York run. All Scousers are said to eat salt fish on Sunday
mornings and very many do. (To get a thirst for the after-Mass
ale?) The couplet was made into a song, by, I believe, Liverpool comic Wally Woods with many other verses. A group
recorded a version and, as they were called The Vipers, I
introducing them in a radio programme naughtily, but (if I
never move from here) spontaneously, said: 'They sound like
a team of Jewish window-cleaners.'

Rationing, 1918

You know Mrs. Brown, There's some sausage in the town,
    Will you have it in yer hand or in yer eye-ee?

Somehow this parody of 'Good Bye-ee' shocked my mother,
who blithely sang:

When We Are Married

When we are married
        We'll have sausage for tea,
Sausage for tea,
When we are, etc. . . .

God Bless Us and Save Us

God bless us and save us,
Said ould Mrs. Davis,
I never knew herrings wuz fish before.

Potatoes and Fishes

Potatoes and fishes,
Is jolly good dishes,
An' Patrick's Day in the morning.

Both imported from Dublin, our sister-city.

Last Night We Had a Do

Last night we had a do,
Some chipped potatoes too . . .

The Cat Sat in the Rice-pan

The cat sat in the rice-pan,
        the rice-pan, the rice-pan,
The cat sat in the rice-pan
        and blamed it on the dog.

Just like a cat. 'Sat' is a euphemism.

V

MID-TERM

Knock at the do-er,
Ring the bell,
Shout down the lobby,
Is yer mother well?

I Went to a Chinese Laundry

I went to a Chinese Laundry,
I asked for a piece of bread,
They wrapped me up in a tablecloth
And sent me off to bed.—Singing,
    Ah Black Sam, the negro
    Abajou, abajou, jay,
    Carader Bungalow Sam.

I saw an Indian maiden,
She stood about ten feet high,
Her hair was painted sky blue pink
And she only had one eye.—Singing,
    Ah Black Sam, the negro
    Abajou, abajou, jay,
    Carader Bungalow Sam.

I saw a pillow box floating
I jumped in rather cool,
It only took me fourteen days
To get to Liverpool.—Singing,
    Ah Black Sam, the negro
    Abajou, abajou, jay,
    Carader Bungalow Sam.

Puzzle over that Kafka-like scene, over sixty years old, supplied by Mr. W. Jaques of Woolton, Liverpool!

Mrs. Lewis of Huyton, Liverpool, says she skipped to this in Dublin 56 years ago. Her chorus slightly varied—such variants prove oral-aural origin to me—making the ending

> Singing Caro bungle air.
> Uncle Sam the Negro,
>> For you don't care, and I don't care,
> Down the Canal Lane.

Off, Off, Off to the Butcher's Shop

Off, off, off to the butcher's shop
I daresn't stay no longer,
'Cos if I did my mother would say
I was playing with the boys down yonder.

Boys and girls in Liverpool spent a deal of their leisure time shopping for their mothers, and adult women still describe shopping as 'doing me messages,' a phrase perfectly normal to me which puzzled and amused a TV producer whom I was helping to make a food-advertising film in the city.

Will You Surrender?

> Will you surrender, will you surrender
>> The King of the Barbaroos?
> We won't surrender, we won't surrender,
>> The King of the Barbaroos!

Something of the sort on B.B.C., 4th March, 1969.

Very old. Could go back to the port's slaveship days. Part of a forgotten boys' game of the Prisoners' Base sort—which we call Rally-o. But don't stop to play, sis, lad or it's . . .

Gee Back

Gee back, woa back,
Go and get yer money back.

You would also have to go back with faulty goods, including
bad eggs, carried openly on a saucer. Mind you, 'doing the
messages' or 'running an erring' had its compensations. How
else, by theft, bribe or tip, raise the penny to buy comics or
go to shows?

Isn't It Funny

Isn't it funny, The cat's got money
And I've got none?

Forward, Doctor Bowdler

Lissen, lissen, the cat's missin'.

A Corporation Muck Cart

A Corporation muck cart was full up to the brim,
The Corporation muckman fell in and couldn't swim
He sank to the bottom just like a little stone
And then we heard him whisper-ing
There's no place like home.

Chacun a son gout.

In 1921

In 1921 all the Zeppelins will be gone
And the Kaiser as well
Will be blown down to Hell.

Survivors of the second scrap can't believe that airships from Germany were a menace in 1917. As to survivors of both— ? May they never know better! The Kaiser died of old age!

Broad A to American Readers

The higher up the mountain
The greener grows the grass.—
The higher up the monkey goes
The more you can see of his ——.

The warning to show-offs my remembrancer Sid Gould of the British Board of Boxing Control must often since have given.

Social Survey 1920

(i)

A bug and a flea
Went out to tea
Upon a reel of cotton,
The bug got lost
The flea was tossed,
    Upon somebody's bottom.

(ii)

Mary Ellen at the pawnshop door,
A bundle on her arm and a bundle on the floor.
She asked for seven bob and they only give her four—
So she knocked the blooming handle off the pawnshop door.

Ta Mrs. Worrel of Wirral. Worrel you ave?

And, 1970, from Holy Cross girls:

(iii)

It's a long way to the pawnshop, It's a long way to go,
It's a long way to the pawnshop, but there you gorra go—
Wid yer father and yer mother And yer baldie-headed
   brother,
It's where the ould ones go.—
There goes me Sunday wicker* And me watch and chain
And you'd better keep yer eye on the drain-pipes Nelly
Or they'll go just the same.
   I tittly i-ti, salt fish.

*Suit. 'Tune Tipperary.'

Mary Brown

Mary Brown went to town
And come back with a nice young man.
They went to stay in the house next door,
Now what will they get married in?

Consumer Report

Mrs. Lees, a box of peas,
Two for tuppence hapenny,
Are they good or are they bad?
—They're not worth a hapenny.

Ask Me No Questions

Ask me no questions,
I'll tell yer no lies—
I seen a Chinaman doing up his
Flies are a nuisance in the summer time.

Thank you, madams.

Felix

Felix kept on walking, kept on walking still,
With his hands between his legs
Feeling for his Easter eggs ——

Per-version of twenties song about the ever-perambulating
film cartoon cat as is following about the older song 'There
was a Jolly Miller'.

With One Hand on the Hopper

With one hand on the hopper
And the other on his chopper——

What will these lads sing, to giggling girls, when they reach
the top class, as big boyses?

Have You Ever?

Have you ever had your hand caught in a mangle?
And some dirty booger comes an' turns the handle?
Your wrist goes flop,
Your hand drops off.
Have you ever had your hand caught in a mangle?

Mrs. Young of Speke, Liverpool, should know, from male
correspondents I have heard of worse accidents.

You Got Trouble?

I had a little monkey worth ten pound,
It washed all the floor and scrubbed all around,
Went upstairs to make its little bed,
Fell into the pisspot

And broke its little head.
Went down in the cellar to get itself a drink,
A bogeyman copped him
And shoved him down the sink.

I Had a Little Doggie

I had a little doggie it was so very small,
It cocked its little leg and wee'd against the wall.
When the wall began to smoke,
It thought it was on fire—
So it cocked its little leg again
—And went a little higher.

Don't Be a Freud Johnnie

Johnnie get your gun,
There's a girl in the garden,
Lying on her belly with her back to the sun.
Johnny got his gun And the gun was loaded—
Stuck it up her bum and
Her bum exploded.

'Ban the bum!'

Mrs. Young of Speke, Liverpool, who gave me that which I
knew and Freudianly forgot also proved how kids' rhymes did
keep up with events. From the thirties:

Will you come to Abysinnia will you come?
With your home and your missus and your gun,
Mussolini will be there
Shooting bullets in the air
Will you etc.?

As Mr. Watkinson of Leyland recalls the visit to Lancs. of
the great Indian patriot in his home-made cotton loincloth:

A certain young fellow named Gandhi
Went in a pub for a shandy (?)
—When he lifted his cloth
To wipe off the froth
The barmaid murmured, 'That's handy!'

I'd Love To Be

I'd love to be a caterpillar,
Life would be a farce.
I'd climb right up a cabbage
And fall down on my hands and knees.

Mr. Ashbridge of Widnes who sent me that has after his name AIMTA, ACCS and I hope they're not rude too.

Saturday Penny

Saturday tomorrow
Buy a penny gun
Run behind a bobby
And shoot him in the bum.

Little Willie

Little Willie lived in Dover,
Little Willie got run over;
Thought it would be rather fun
In the crowded street to run.
That was the end of little Willie—
He shouldn't have been so flipping silly.

I hope Meiron Roberts forgives my slight change.

There was a little man
And he had a little gun

And over the brick fields he did run
With a big straw hat
And a belly full of fat
And a pancake tied to his bum.

In First World War the pre-1914 'straw hat' became 'tin hat'.

Many as well as Mrs. Houston of Liverpool 7 remember this.

Tom Boy

(Regina Cunningham says her grandma taught her this when she was 5.)

When I was a nipper,
A giddy little kipper,
A feller once said to me.
'I know where there's a tree
Loaded up with fruit—
Wouldn't it just suit,
Anybody small?'

So off I went to have a look at 'em
And just got my leg upon the wall,
When my blood ran pale
'Cos a six-inch nail,
Stuck right up you know where
    the monkey's got a tail—
And I never got to look at 'em at all.

'I Don't Want To Be Made a Man Of, Sergeant!'

As late as 1914 they were recruiting at the senior school doorstep. Many an idle hobbledehoy was caught as he moodied round the streets at vacation time.

When I was young I used to be
Bandy-legged and knocky knee,
The Prince of Wales (!) he come to me
To go and join the Armee.

Chinese Alphabet

Chi chi chick a li
Chick a li romi
Rinkim pinkim pan
Para para whisket gee
Hip a Qu, Chi Cho Chee.

Ta Mrs. Joan Bennet. The next is from Stan Hugill.

A ran jigger ran
Poony, Poony, Ping Pong Ping
Agga, backa, susie racka
Um tum tush.

'True folk' says Stan.

As I was going down the street
I bought a penny whistle
A bobby took it off me
And give me a lump a gristle,
I asked him for it back.
He said he hadn't got it,
I said 'You are a liarty,
You got it in your pocket.'

'You're a liarty' as a yodel often among twenties kids.

Give Us a Penny

Give us a penny
To go to the Delly
To see Mrs. Kelly
With a wart on her belly.

The seventy-one year old Lollipop man—in Everton, a former clergyman, who started life in an Everton ragged school sang that as a lad at the Delly, in Christian Street, where F.S.'s father appeared, in green tights, as a wrestler, Jack Murphy—he was Welsh, Murphy was his wife's maiden name. By the time the Great War One came it was a cinema and boys who couldn't bunk in—free entry being as much part of a Liverpool poor-class lad's life as stealing from the docks— locust beans, togo sugar, anything—could still enter for a penny. On their way home they'd sing the next one and be greeted by their mother with 'How dare youse go to the Delly and yer father in the Dardanelles?'

Mrs. Kelly of the rhyme could be the actress wife of W. W. Kelly, flamboyant local impressario (If you ever saw him without a carnation you received a sovereign they said— nobody ever got it). He wrote and she performed in the famous Royal Divorce in which *did not* occur the famous line 'Not tonight Josephine!'

F.S.'s dad said the Delly had a notice on its wall: 'Ladies in bare feet not admitted'.

'Little Redwing'

The moon shines tonight on Charlie Chaplin,
  His boots are crackin'
  For the want of blackin'
An' his khaki trousis they want mendin'
Before we send 'im to the Dardanelles.

The original song about the Injun maid is long forgotten. The parody is as immortal as Charlie, then new on the screeen with Elaine, of the Exploits, and Keystone comedies; not to mention The Clutching Hand, The Laughing Mask, Eddie Polo, Stingaree.

  Flickering on the screen to the music of the Delly pianist, who while rattling out chase music or Hearts and Flowers, or good patriotic stuff, whipped one hand to his bowler on the piano lid in which was a packet of chips. We stood up to make shadows on the screen while the chucker-out, with a big stick like a baseball bat, shouted, 'Get sat down youse!'

Screen and stage gave, in the twenties, two other parodies which outlived the originals, 'I'd Like to Sleep with Nazimova' (Whispering) and 'Peggy O'Neill is a girl you can feel'. In his 1969 version, Danny La Rue sang the proper words.

Billy Ritchie

The moon shines bright on Billy Ritchie
His feet is itchy, Like little Titchy . . .

There were many imitators of Chaplin, not entirely original himself, though, like Shakespeare, he brought borrowing to the height of genius. One was a former boxer named Billy Ritchie who was even featured in British comic papers as Charlie (*The Essanay Comic*) was.

'The Moon Shines Bright' was a kid's creation, one of the great parodies, almost certainly originating in the 'Pool. But those who think, as some have written, it was the last invention of rhymes by kids, are quite wrong, as I have told *the* experts, Mr. and Mrs. Opie. For example, from a school in the Prime Minister's constituency (in 1969) in the fifties the next two, followed by a 1968 creation from a city infants' school, preserved by the ever-watchful and helpful Lena Bergen, headmistress.

The Cruel 3C

I was standin' on the corner wid me cosh an' chain
When up comes a scuffer* and asses me me name,
I pulls back the corner uv me gaberdeen coat
Whips out me razor and slashes his t'roat.

*Policeman.
The use of bicycle chains, coshes and such weapons by the

Liverpool 'buckos' was something new. They had never fought fair, butting and 'the boot' being usual, but—no weapons.

Radio Tec, Remember?

The crook stood on the burning deck
    While Snowy* blew his hooter,
And who'd d'you think come round the bend?
    Dick Barton on a scooter.

*Snowy, his assistant.

Ab Ora Infantum

My dog is black
My dog is a retriever
My dog had pups (!)
My dog's got spikes on its stummik.

This observant little girl was aged eight; the elders took her chant up readily, i.e. kids of nine or ten.

The Wheels of Chance

Does yer mother ride a bike
Wid her fingers on the handlebars?
An' her fingers in her thing
An' the clappers of her ass
Going ting a ling a ling?

This, absolutely new to compilers, Bill Moore, Merseyside folk singer, heard at school in the thirties, but it clearly goes back to biking craze of the turn of the century. What a memory that lad has! He recalled to the tune of 'Dare to be a Daniel'.

Dare to Go Down Scotty Road

—but nobody else does! And he only the one line.

Micky Roche

Micky Roche* is no good,
Chop him up for fi-erwood,
    When he's dead
    Bile his head,
Then we'll all have gingerbread.

*Or any other temporary enemy. I once heard a local boxer,
middle-aged, half-drunk, on a late tram, as he swung on the
strap, singing this softly about a one-time opponent.

Retort to 'I'll Tell Miss'

Tell her, tell her, knock her down the cellar
    Wid a old umbereller.

Retort to 'What?'

Pot. Eat it while it's 'ot.

Reply to 'Where've You Been?'

As far as there and back ageen.

Chanted but of course the verse is really blank. So was my
mind as in me long stockings and Paddy-'at, straight from the
bogs, unfamiliar with the Scouse tone, I first heard these.
Some I heard won me, still not comprehending, when repeated, a belting. *Reprisal:* Eh, you, come back?—Yis, what

d'yer want ?—To know 'ow far you'd a gone if I aden a called
yer back!

> I went to the pitchers tomorrow
> I gorra front seat at the back;
> I bought a plain cake wid currents in—
> I ate it and gave it him back.

—1917.

The Opies surprised me by finding this elsewhere. Doubtless
I'm in for more surprises.

Readers who recalled this outside Liverpool staggered me
by their numbers. They brought too those variants I love.
Keith Taylor of Bridlington (Yorkshire) after getting his seat
at the back

A lady gave me some chocolate, I ate it, etc.

> I fell from the floor to the ceiling
> And broke a front bone in my back.
> They laid me on a stretcher,
> I stretched out in a bed,
> They rubbed my belly
> With a lump of jelly,
> And this is what I said—

A Glaswegian got an apple from the lady, Mr. D. Whittle
of Bolton after taking his seat has an astonishing new gloss,
making me feel as if the Dead Sea Scrolls turned out to be a
railway guide:

> I fell from the pit to the gallery
> And broke a front bone in my back.

He went up a street down, a bark dogged at him so he picked
up a throw and stone it.

This lacks the quality of the next one which, with Billy Nitt
(the chemistry master) of Chapter II, the 'Mystery Carol' at
the end of that chapter and 'What will we wash in ?' of the
Ink Pink chap were used in a 'Liverpool Street Cantata' by

George MacBeth for Novello Publishing Co., London, the Scouse voices being Roger McGough, poet, Adrian Henri, ditto. The Cantata was presented at the Madeley Teachers Training College, Staffs. and on the Stoke-on-Trent Radio in May 1970 and the same songs with others were on Radio Merseyside in June 1970 sung by the Holy Cross school-children.

John Brown's Body

John Brown's baby's got a pimple on its,
John Brown's baby's got a pimple on its ad infin.

More Nonsense

One fine September morning
October in July,
The sun lay thick upon the ground,
The flowers were singing gaily;
The birds were in full bloom
When I went down in the cellar
To clear the back bedroom;
I saw ten thousand miles away
A house right out of sight,
It stood alone between two others
And it was black-washed white.

One gets a sort of new and wild sense as with 'The Twelve Nights of Christmas' and 'A Host of Furious Fancies'. My informant, Mrs. Bond of Huyton, says she copied it out in 1947, but it is much older. As is the well-known—

One fine day in the middle of the night
Two dead men got up to fight.

Which ends with—
A man fell into a bucket of ice-cold water
And scalded himself dreadfully.

But though he dies he's still 'a little better in the morning.'

Kids loved this sort of thing where dead men fight and dumb men speak and black is white and whatever astronauts say, the moon is made of green cheese and cows jump over it and Sally goes round it. They love also the unending rhyme and keep on with this oral equivalent to the mathematical pi to the verge of hysteria for the adult. They also like 'The House that Jack Built' sort. The examples of both which follow, not before, I believe, written down, were among the nursery rhymes like 'Trinity church I met my doom' and 'Some very funny things took place in our back-yard last night, An elephant trod on me sister's face, In our . . .'—given me by my dad in my cot in Tralee about 1912. I spread them in Liverpool. Before rendering these bizarre lullabies the singer introduced himself as 'The man who fought the monkey in the dust-hole and come out without a scratch.'

A Dramatic Monologue

'Twas a storm and darky night
        The rain came down in torrents,
The brigand chief and all his gang were there.
Said the brigand chief to Antonio:
'Antonio, tell us a story.'
        Antonio began as follows—
'Twas a storm and darky night . . .

Ad infin. He couldn't go on long enough for me. But he would interrupt himself with such enigmas as Don't judge a poor man by the corns on his face.

—1900.

By Way of An Onkore

(A likkle song entitled 'When The Sheets
Are Short The Bed Seems Longer')

The Wild Man of Borneo has just come to town, just
come to town, just come to town—
The Wife of the Wild Man of Borneo has just come
to town . . .
The Child of the Wife of the Wild Man of Borneo has
just come to town . . .
The Dog of the Child of the Wife of the Wild Man of
Borneo has just come to town . . .
The Ear of the Dog of the Child of the Wife of the
Wild Man of Borneo has just come to town . . .
The Flea in the Ear of the Dog of the Child of the
Wife of the Wild Man of Borneo has just come to town . . .
1900.

Any Gum Chum?

Where you goin', Joe? Down the lane, Joe.
Wat for, Joe? Mojo.* Let's come, Joe. No, Joe. Why, Joe?
Because you'll steal the Mojo.

*A species of chewing-gum, from an African word of varied,
not always polite, meaning. Not because of that, but because
I suppose of its use and disposal (Old Song: 'Does the chewing-
gum lose its flavour on the bedpost overnight?'; we used
under the desk). They said it was bad for us, like so many
things we liked, like 'fades', rotting apples, sold cheap. In
my wife's school little girls swore that on a grave-stone in
Ford 'Symmetry' was a stone bearing the inscription—

Chewing gum, chewing gum, made of wax,
Has brought me to my grave at last.

Surely the worst rhyme yet. The kids in last war begging the GI's for 'Any gum, chum?' were not as mercenary as we. As, to the cheers of females long since starved of the sight of fit young males, they lolloped from the Landing Stage trooper to Knotty Ash—in a graveyard there are many of them still, victims of the virulent Spanish Flu of 1918-19—cowboy-hatted, packs bumping against their lean sterns, our cry was, 'Any cents, Sam?' We repaid their generosity by adding our own verse to their 'Inky pinky parly voo'.

> The Yanks are having a jolly good time, parly voo.
> The Yanks are having a jolly good time, parly voo.
> The Yanks are having a jolly good time
>   Kissing the Waacs behind the line,
> Inky pinky parlyvoo.

No doubt picked up from older boys, maybe in the British Services where, in both wars, our gallant if belated allies were not exactly gushed over. Perhaps another word for 'kissing' was used but this word, now heard from the lips of high-born ladies, and due any week now in the pages of *Kiddies Own*, was not common among us rough lads or, in our hearing, our male elders.

> Over the top and the best of luck,
> If you don't come back we'll know you're stuck,
> With a W—A—A—C.

The next adapted from a popular song, one of those un-ending things, is kinder. Cleaner?

Around the Corner

Around the corner behind a tree, behind a tree,
A Yankee soldier he said to me:
When're you gunna marry me I should like to know
'Cos every time I look in your eyes I feel I wanna go—
Around the corner . . . etc.

Dramatic Interlude

First Boy: Who's in the water?
Second Boy: King's daughter.
First Boy: Who'll save her?
Second Boy: I will.
First Boy: You will, and who are you?
Both (quickly): I'm jolly Jack the Sailor, just come home from
    sea. (*Simulated horn-pipe music based on*—)
Tiddlywinks, old man, Get a woman if you can,
If you can't get a woman, Get a clean old man.

                             (alternatively—)

. . . a corned beef can.

    Definitely, in both cases, from older brothers who also
favoured the other interlude 'This being my daughter's
wedding day' and a medley of song titles which seeped down
to us in short trousers kicking a clump of rag along the cobbles
or playing Heavy On Ton Weight against a warehouse wall or
playing 'Ollies' (marbles) or its variants with buttons and
cherry-stones (cherry-wobs or -wogs).

Medley of Song Titles

When Irish eyes are smilin'
Are we downhearted? No.
It's a long way to Tipp'raree
For her eyes have told me so.
She came into the world with nothing,
Bonny Mary of Argyle
And she wore a wreath of roses—
Around her Emerald Isle.

                                 c. 1919.

Two More

From Stalybridge 'over the water' Mrs. Hirst sent this and
the one to follow, roughly same period, mid-twenties, from
Doncaster shows similar ingenuity.

> Show me the way to go home
> I love my Chilly Bom Bom,
> In the eyes of the world you belong to me,
> California, Here I Come.
> It ain't gonna rain no more,
> Oh, darling, do say Yes,
> I'm the Sheik of Araby—
> Out of the Golden West.
>
> When Irish eyes are smilin'
> Put me in a taxi, Joe,
> And drop me nice and handy
> Where the black-eyed Susans grow,
> Somewhere a voice is calling,
> To Mary of Argyle,
> Who was born with a wreath of roses
> And the sunshine of a smile.

Each line here isn't a song title and some were well before
twenties.

Mother, Mother

> Mother, Mother, take me home
> From this Convalescent Home,
> I've been here a week or two
> Now I want to be with you,
> Goodbye all the nurses, goodbye Sister too,
> Goodbye to all the doctors and Convalescent home.

(Rhyme could have been bettered, the sincerity never.)

Doctor Dyson

Doctor Dyson (?), give me my discharge,
For you know I want to go,
Why don't you tell me so?
Give me back my liberty, for I want to see
A little girl with curly hair, It's dear old home for me.
Goodbye, goodbye, farewell to you
Goodbye to Liquorice, Black Jack too,
Goodbye to Doctor Dawson
And the end of the corridor, too.

After the black-jack you had to run down the corridor; then as now nurses were obsessed with bowel movements. This song from the ward and not the street recalls like 'Goodbye Mary' in 'Ink Pink' chapter the dreaded fever van of pre-1914 days. The lady who sent it to me was eight months in the children's ward singing it every day. Visits were rare, food inadequate, discipline high.

Ten, Twenty, Thirty, Forty, Fifty Years Ago

This medley, brought to our Liverpool 'college' about 1924 by the son of a well-known local theatre impressario who grew up to be Canon Paul Montgomery, had a great, though brief, vogue with us 'puddens':

Maxwelton's braes are bonny
Where stands the Gra-and Hotel
And 'twas there I got an egg for my breakfast
And I knew as I opened the shell
That was an egg of the old brigade,
And I don't suppose that egg had been laid
For months and months and months.

Annie Laurie and the other two songs being followed by

many more of a vintage as old as the egg.—We loved the pause
before the waitress's arrival—

> Egg—shells—she—saw.

Poor old Longfellow!

A Few Street Parodies

(Could have had adult inspiration or assistance but I don't
think so.)

(i)

When the whispering swines in the parlour.

> ('When the whispering pines of Nevada')

(ii)

Down Richmond Row where they pay no rent.
When the Landlord comes
They say the rent is spent.
Knock him down wid the poker.
Lay him out upon the sofa—

> ('Down Texas Way')

(iii)

Wherever you may roam
To the Delly or the Sailors Home
It's no disgrace. To go to Melville Place—
Show me the way to go home.

1924, before General Strike. 'Delly,' not cinema, posh
central hotel, Adelphi; Melville Place was the Board of
Guardians' Headquarters ('The Parish').

(iv)

Bummin' for ale, boys, bummin' for ale,
First into Walker's then into Cain's.

Two brewers, later amalgamated, are recalled in this parody
of the hymn 'This Is My Story'. Cp. woeful 'carol' No ale,
no ale.

An old seadog for a hard road, Stan Hugill went further,

> Sometimes we get it,
> Sometimes we fail,
> Then into Threlfalls and back again.

Threlfall's. One of this brewer's pubs, Tom Hall's, now demolished in the Goree near Pier Head, was known to seamen all over the world. You know, all the landscape improvement by bulldozer Liverpool has had to endure in the no-doubt laudable aim to make it like any other provincial city and destroy the idiosyncratic one this book itself reflects, objection to which is so strong that there is talk of Arthur Dooley chaining himself to the Town Hall railings, makes me one with the eccentric millionaire newspaper proprietor in the USA who, after a successful attempt to prevent automatic telephones coming to his Western town, triumphantly headlined the news 'Progress Resisted'.

Remember and honour the name, Lucius Beebe.

Tickling Song

> There was a likkle nigger an'
> He wouldn't say his prayers, so
> We put him in a bandbox an'
> Threw him down the stairs.
> The stairs give a crack an'
> Broke his likkle back an'
> All the likkle ducks went—

(Older brother or sister's fingers twitch and baby, who's had it all before, squirms in anticipation, as very quickly—)
> Quack, Quack, Quack.

I'm afraid you can't keep 'niggers' out of the kids' songs, from 'Ten Little Nigger Boys' on, but kids are no racialists and many of us brought a penny which would have bought two comics or two ounces of milky choo choo to the school mission fund—in our school we put it into a manually-operated collection box of which the slot was Sambo's mouth. Yes, Sambo. For a 'black baby.' Some of the black babies we bought now doubtless are Cabinet Ministers or beating us hollow at Olympic Games.

In Liverpool we've lived too long with the blacks—and Chinky Chinky Chinamen—and Taffy (who was a thief)—and Paddy Irish—to think of them in anything but fraternal terms.

Really, we even like the bobbies!

'Contents' Backwards

Suck Tommy's Nose Eat Tommy's Nose Oh Cripes
Some Teachers Never Enter Till Nine O' Clock

Another forwards one was (says Bill Cogley)—

Cows Ought Not To Eat Nuts Till Sunday
c. 1948. A relation recalls alternative—
Cows Ought Not To Eat Nasty Turnip Stalks

—All to be chanted almost Gregorically.

'Over the Water'

Wallasey for wreckers,
Poulton for trees,
Leasowe for honest men
And Seacombe for thieves.

Recalled by Merseyside Nomad, writer and broadcaster (Norman Ellison).

For us, even when they bred rhymes like 'trees' and 'thieves' they were all beautiful.

To go over the water, on the school picnic to Eastham Woods by ferry, a bag of rock cakes and a bottle of mineral to keep us going all day, crowded on the Cheshire-side train (Teacher: Last year a boy put his head out of a carriage window and it was chopped right off), marching maybe miles through the Liverpool streets to the 'Lanny.' As to Masefield to us the Mersey was 'beautiful at all times.' Best was the penny ferry, with mam (youngest kids free) to Seacombe and the walk to New Brighton ('Don't forget the diver'—a one-legged man our own Tommy Handley recalled in ITMA). 'Come unto these yellow sands.' They were yellow then. We had a gear time. Many years after a local comic told me how, waiting tensely to set off on the Normandy landings, the inevitable wag cheered up the Liverpool Kings by rolling his trousers up, getting a shovel and a bucket and running along shouting 'Come on, lads, we're going over the water wid me mam!' When I first crossed with me dad I cried. I thought we were leaving England, which I already loved. Ah, the Joy Wheel has lost its joy, The House on Nonsense has become a world, the topless tower of New Brighton was topped. . . . And the ice cream, with the buckshee jet of raspberry, long since melted.

An Arab's Farewell to His Street

On the Rhyl Promenade
On the top of a ladder
There's a feller in the middle
—Wid a head like a bladder.

Trip recalled by that lollipop man. The title was Alf Linnet's about a mission hall outing to New Brighton and street-kids sang the song. But it was written in Cockney!

In Harold Wilson's Constituency

Huyton, Huyton, two dogs fightin'
One a black an' one a white 'un.

Old, maybe eighteenth century, as is—

> Prescot, Huyton and merry Childow,
> Three parish churches all in a row,
> Prescot for mugs, Huyton for ployes,
> Childwall for ringing and singing beside.

Prescot made panmugs and other crockery, Childwall had an ancient religious house 'the Abbey'; would Huyton's ployes be gimmicks or, as in Stephen Potter's gamesmanship, gambits? Umm!

Wandering Minstrel, Liverpool 1916

> Where'er I go I take my po
> And a little bit of last night's Echo'o . . .
> > So slip on yer likkle jersey
> > Come down the River Mersey
> And bunkaloodilido wit' me.

> Where are the lads of the villidge tonight
> Where are the nuts* we knew?
> They've gone to shoot the Kayser
> Fr sinking the Lusitanier.
> > That's where they are tonight.

*Young elegants, spelt 'knuts'.

As Glyn Hughes' Seth Davey had delighted our dads— 'Come day, go day, the Lord send Sunday' and their grandchildren delighted in the juke boxes' reiteration of the Beatles' 'Penny Lane,' we kids of the first World War loved the banjoist who gave us this version, which we repeated and repeated, as we did our messages, shouted after people, annoyed shopkeepers by asking them for food they hadn't got (one, at Bell and Barnett's, was nicknamed 'No sugar, No sugar'),—'Any empty boxes?'—'Well fill them' (this, from one boy, in an undertaker's); 'Any broken biscuits?'—'Well, mend 'em'; stole, played, fought and scrounged coppers. We liked his Billy Merson parodies such as the Echo and Mersey sketch but he was best with his adaptation of the Darewski song 'Where Are The Boys?' Alternative endings:

> They're up to their knees in water
> To stop the German slaughter—

Dat's Whur Dey Are Tonight

A note on kids and war, songwise, fits in here.

In the First World War, at least in the early years, we in Liverpool were much more patriotic than in this and certainly so (I am told) in the Boer War: it has something to do with how closely the citizen is involved. In both the Boer and 1914 do some of this flowed into the kids. Kids had always liked to be dressed as sailors; in 1914 they were dressed as soldiers. (The dockers even, later, went into khaki.) In both the leading figures Bobs, Baden Powell, Fighting Jack, Kitchener, French, Jellico were worshipped like modern footballers by the boys in the street and we derided Kaiser Bill with his son Little Willy and ould von Kluck as our dads did ould Kruger and de Wet but it didn't go deep. We had loads of patriotic stuff, including songs, in the classroom—my own kids seemed to miss this in 1939—but 'Boys in khaki, boys in blue, Here's a jolly good luck to you' and ''Twas the night of the charge, And the Lancashire's stood with bay'nets bright and grim' (given to us by a Lancashire war widow—what did we know of Lancashire? Our lads were with the Eighth Irish, Kings and such) or the anthems including the Russian's (then the majestic 'God the all-terrible') didn't flow into the school-yard. We had parodies such as, from serving brothers—

> Oh, it's a luvly war . . .
> I luv my wife,
> I love her dearly,
> I love . . .

> Your King and country need you,
> Why the devil don't they feed you?

But the Lads of the Village only one I recall sung in earnest.
It was 'Bubbles' on Armistice Day! The student of folk song,
Carl Engel (1818–82) has noted the difference which is not
always observed between 'volklied,' a national song, and a
merely popular song 'volkthumlicheslied'. Ach himmel, Carl,
you said it. Our secular and sacred music oft confused too, I
fear. Folk song should keep out of the streets—and trenches.
As the other German critic, Herder (1744–1803), breaking
eggs with a big stick (to quote me Dad) said 'It is no reproach
to the noblest of poetry to say that it is heard on the lips of the
common people.' But (he adds) 'we do not mean those in the
streets and alleys who never sing or make poetry, but only yell
and destroy.' I say that the rural folk tradition is now being
artificially preserved, when not actually given a heart trans-
plant from us alley-rats, and a real folk tradition has stayed and
grown naturally in our streets and playgrounds. In what
follows there is often great poetry and true song and the child
is father and mother to the man/woman.

VI

INK, PINK, PEN AND INK
(Counting and Skipping)

All along the line a docks
Sellin' matches penny a box.

One, Two, Three

One, two, three, Billy Magee caught a flea
And put it in his mother's tea,
When his mother found out,
She give him a clout.

Fleas were as familiar as bobbies and as funny as shirts. (Bill Cogley's version of rhyme used earlier.)

One, two, three, a leara,
I saw me Anty Sarah
Sitting on her bumalaira,
Eating choc'late babies.

Enough work for three Freuds round some of these songs. I don't know what 'a leara' means in this ball-bouncing-'Cock yer leg over,' game but I don't accept 'O'Leary' in the 1968 'hit' song. Word vaguely Celtic though.

Eeper, Weeper, chimbley sweeper
Had a wife and couldn't keep her.
Got another, didn't love her,
Up the chimbley he did shove her.

I Went Up One Stair,

I went up two stairs

I saw a monkey.

You reply—Just like me,

—Just like me,

and so on to

—You can't ketch me.

Manchester Races, Buttermilk Cream

This was a swift skipping game, 'Pitch, patch, pepper.' Liverpool girls were proficient skippers. Even adult women outside the factory would stretch a rope the width of the street and have a turn. You can't get the real 'skelp' without the cobblestones.

Thirteen-year old Susan Wheatley sent the next six with Chin, chin, Chinaman.

> Blue bells, cockle shells,
> Eeevery, ivory, over, Daddy is a butcher.
> (*Skipping*) Mother cuts the meat.
> How many hours does the baby sleep?
> Five, ten, fifteen, twenty ...
>   Oh, me Uncle Mick
> He had a big stick
> And he took it to the slaughter
> He killed two thousand Orangemen—
> At the battle of the Boiling Water.*
> Pitch, patch, pepper ...

*Boyne?

> Grandma, grandma Gray,
> May I go out to play?
> I won't go near the waterside
> To scare the ducks away.
> Pitch, patch.

> Our Susan is a funny 'un
> With face like a pickled onion,

A nose like a squashed tomato
And two props for legs.—Miss the rope,
   you're out.
I like coffee, I like tea (*Skipping*)
I don't like Janet In-with-me.

Add together the numbers on bus tickets:

One for sorrow, Two for joy,
Three for a girl, Four for a boy;
Five for silver, Six for gold,
Seven for a secret—Never to be told;
Eight for a wish, Nine for a kiss
And ten for a disappointment.

Now, even with the 'wish'–'kiss' rhyme, who thought of
that lovely thing first?

One, two, three, four, five, six, seven,
All good children go to heaven.

From even younger Pauline Heffey (7), whose handwriting
at least is childish! She lives in 55 Northway, Liverpool 15, if
you want to write to her.

Humpty Dumpty sat on the wall
Eating a bunch of bananas.
Where do you think he put the skin?
Down his best pyjamas.

And this

Micky Mouse is dead.
He killed himself in bed.
He cut his throat with a ten-pound note
And this is what he said.—
Red white and blue,
My mother was a Jew,

My father was an Englishman,
So out go YOU. (?)

Plus

As I was walking down Piggy Wiggy Lane
I smelt a box of kippers.
I asked a lady what it was,
She said she'd wet her knickers.
    Pitch, patch, pepper.

Charlie Chaplin went to France
To teach the ladies how to dance,
Heel, toe, over we go,
Right about turn.

Recalled by Mrs. Chadwick of Leeds with

I am a Girl Guide dressed in blue,
These are the actions I can do,
Salute the King, Bow to the Queen
And turn my back on Kaiser Bill.

Both *c.* 1915

Fie, fie for shame
Turn your back to the wall again
And tell your sweetheart's name.
Billy Moore says he'll have her,
All the boys are fighting for her.
Let them all say what they like,
Billy Moore has a wife.

This addendum to 'Wallflowers, Wallflowers' a surprise to
me especially as the girl had a wedding ring to start with!

Jumbo, Jumbo sitting in the dust-hole,
Eating mouldy cheese.
One, two—A rat came by,
Hit him in the eye,

And made old Jumbo sneeze,
      One, two, etc.

Sixty years old, says Ann Johnson of Huyton, Liverpool.
At least.

Chin Chin Chinaman

Chin chin Chinaman
Bought a penny doll,
He washed it and dressed it
And called in Pretty Poll.
He sent for the doctor
The doctor couldn't come
Because he had a pimple on his bum, bum, bum.

Porky Flynn

Porky Flynn is a fool,
Tied his stockings to a stool,
When the stool began to crack
All the bugs ran up his back.

Remember 'I chased a bug around a room, I'll have his
blood 'ee knows I will'?

Out Goes She

I know a washer-woman,
I invited her to tea,
'Have a cup of tea, mam.' 'No, mam.'
'Why, mam?' 'Where, mam?' 'Here mam.'
'In me big toe, mam.'—OUT GOES SHE.

Ickerty pickerty Iserlicketty, pamperlaree jig,
Every man that has no hair ought to wear a wig.
One, two, three, OUT SHE GOES.

Sando fibber macko da, Do do dacca do fa
Me pretty maid, One two three,
OUT GOES SHE.

Penny on the water, penny on the sea,
Threepence on the railway
And OUT GOES SHE.

There Come Three Jews

There come three Jews, three Jews from Spain
Who came to court my daughter Jane.
My daughter Jane is just too young,
I cannot hear your flatt'ring tongue.
I'll turn and go. Oh, come back, no.—

Pebbles Game

See how many fleas are in your hair.
(*Quick flick of wrist and several are caught on the back of the hand. Another flick.*)
How many in my hair?
(*None, triumphant yell.*)
See, there's none in mine.

Mrs. Wotherspoon, our girls usually used those cubes of stone or baked clay called 'jacks' with marbles in the game 'Jacks and Ollies.'—One of the world's oldest games.

Bolton's Mrs. Foddy heard as a babe—she was 77 in 1969 —this, dated by the hat:

Up yonder hill a far way off
The wind near blew
My billycock off.

Come back and choose the fairest of the lot.
The fairest one that I can see
Is pretty little Jenny.
Won't you come to me?—No.
Dirty young slut you won't come out,
You won't come out, won't come out.
The pretty young slut won't come out—
This fine day.

(*Others join*)

Now we've got a merry ring, a merry ring,
Now we've got a merry ring
This fine day.

The Droylsden (Manchester) lady who sent this strange item added:

The wind, the wind, the wind blows high,
The rain comes tumbling down the sky,
She is handsome, she is pretty,
She's the girl from London city.
She goes a counting one, two, three.
Pray and tell me who is she?
Will you have a lick of that,
Will you have a lick of this,
No sir, no sir, no sir, no,
I'd rather have a kiss.

Gin a Body

If a fellow meets a fellow in a field of fitches would a fellow tell a fellow where a fellow itches. How many EFs?

The Liverpool lady, now living in Southport, Miss Wooley, who sent me the Daddy Bunchy game along with 'there was a man a man indeed Sowed a garden full of seed' with Eeeper, Jeeper, chimney sweeper, Grandmother Gray, and others I shan't use, recalls the rhymes of games, as follow, and 'no chicken herself' says her mother played many of them in the city street.

Ring Game

Oh dear Doctor, can you tell
What will make poor Eva well?
Eva's sick and going to die,
That will make poor Eddy cry.
Eddy's here and Eddy's there,
Eddy's on the water,
Eddy's got the prettiest girl,
Mrs. (Name her)'s daughter.

Clapping Game

The woods are dark
The grass is green
Here comes Johnnie
With his tambourine.

All Together

All together, frosty weather,
I see Peter sitting on the window-sill.
Caroline, Caroline, shoot.

On 'shoot' Mrs. Wooley recalls everyone ran out of skipping-rope. And her mother sang:

Is that you, Sambo?
No, it am Jim.
Well, you can't come in,
You're not good looking,
You can't come in
So please stop knocking at the door.

O-U-T

She goes out like a dirty dish clout,
Lift up the latch and walk straight out.

'Are You Ready for a Fight?'
(Chasing game)

*Two lines face each other, some yards apart, a line marked
down middle, first line advances singing:*
Are you read for a fight? We are the Romans.
Others: Yes, we're ready for a fight, We are the English,
We are ready for a fight, We are the English soldiers.
Etc. ending in a chase.

This must have something to do with 'We Are The English
Army' mentioned in Chapter I. Must be quite old.

On the Swing

As the swing stops:
Die, die, let the cat die,
I went to my grandmother's garden
And picked up a rusty farthing,
I gave it to my mother
To buy me a brother,
'Gainst Sun-day morning.
Final swing:
And a good toss over the boundary green.

The Great Big Ship

The great big ship
Went through the alley-o.
On the fourteenth of December.

This lovely little rhyme, akin to 'Sally Wears a Blue Ribbon',

'Over the Hills and Far Away', 'Down by the Riverside', 'Jenny at the Cottage Door', can, like most beauties, cause almost fratricidal war. 'Alley-o' is French *Allier*? Old British possession Irrawaddy-o?   Oy, Oy!

All agree Liverpudlian Frankie Vaughan's refined version umpty. I think the long residence of Napeleonic War prisoners near our Scotland Road area could have had some influence on our songs—and more. In Great Howard Street was their prison now a hospital. Irish *liked* French, neutral against English. My first nursery rhyme, aged four, 'Some say the divil is dead and buried in Killarney, Others say he rose again an' jined the Inglish Armee.'

Holy Cross girls, 1970, who can hardly have seen the ship, which is registered in Liverpool, but can have relations sailing from Southampton on her (who hasn't?) prefer:

The great big ship was the *Queen E-lizzerbit* clearly enunciating each syllable, emphasising final consonant. Date still 'fourteenth of December'.

'The great big ship went through the alley-o' was the heading to a *Sunday Mirror* (North) picture of the giant tanker *Melo* sailing up the Mersey. Late the evening before publication the Editor had rung the compiler saying, 'Eh, what's that song about a great big ship in your rhyme book, mate?' The girls of Holy Cross R.C. School in Marybone, a Liverpool South Docks school near the site where in false legend Saint Pat himself lodged before sailing for Ireland, sang this, with many more from this book and one other of their own, most beautifully and unaffectedly. They were led by a most human and able teacher, Mrs. Furlong, of the amateur drama group in the 'Pool, Irish Players. The kids were most lucid but she imposed no false gentility on them. I can see the point when teachers get on to me for encouraging them to speak Scouse. I had a long debate on a TV programme with one speech specialist who had made recordings to learn the judies in a district where unemployment was rife to say, if I never move from here, 'My papah has a jaguah'; I'm afraid I interrupted with 'For Jeyes's sake half the kids' dads can't afford a bike!' I suppose the Queen's and Prince Philip's English is best but we want no Cockney refinement nor B.B.C. lawr and orduh stuff. Do let us be natural. After all I understand that many 'speech teachers' are being besieged by Standard-speaking out-of-work actors to teach them Scouse—which, said an Eton headmaster on the air, is the biggest single influence at his school. . . . Holy Cross girls did jib at saying 'seen' for 'saw' so I let it go—especially as they said 'sawr'. I know, I know, it's a collection of *rhymes*.

Infantile Ecumenism

I one the Pope, I two the Pope, until,
I seven the Pope, I 'ate the Pope——

The Big Ship's Name was the 'Lusitania'

On the fourteenth of December,
My father was the captain of the *Lusitania*
On the fourteenth of December.
When the ship went down,
The German sank the *Lusitania*
On the fourteenth of December.

They didn't. It was on 7th May, 1915. There must be some reason for that December date in song much earlier, of course, than the sinking.

See 'Where Are the Boys', previous chapter.

A Very Poor Excuse, Mary Ellen

We wuz on'y playin' leapfrog,
We wuz on'y playin' leapfrog——.

On the Rocks

Eh, laddie, lee, will you come to Shorry Park
And run around the rocks with me?

Recalled by Ormskirk pensioner Johnny Kerr; I knew
Shaw Street Park and often played on the rocks there; it is
now a well-organised children's playground. Still, those
rocks—!

Park was plagued by men our parents warned us against.
Have I grown to be one?

Down by the Riverside

Down by the riverside the green grass grows
    And there little Mary washes her clothes,
She danced and she sung so sweet
She called her sweetheart down the street.
    Sweetheart, sweetheart, will you marry me?
Next Monday morning the wedding will be,
Iced cakes and cheese cakes are all for tea,
We shall have a baby at half past three.

Bless their innocent little hearts many of them could, from
observation in street and home, have taught Miss the Facts.
One of our loveliest, recalling faintly our rural past recalled,
with others, by artist and broadcaster Mrs. Leah Blackman of
Allerton whose memory goes back to city streets over sixty
years ago. She is an expert not only on our songs but games,
sweets, trade, street cries, a delight to talk to.

One Hammer on the Block

Mimers, Mimers,*
One hammer on the block,
Mimer's man,

Rapperty can, blow Billy blow,
    Turn away, boys, for an hour or so.
Two hammers on the block, etc.
Three hammers on the block, etc., etc. . . .

*Dwarf smith—Scandinavian mythology?
Mime—giant of Nibelungelied?

    Palm Sunday, Easter day,
    Carl Sunday, Carl away.

Carl—'man', 'it'?

    Who'll come into my little ring
    To make it a little bigger?
    (*Dancing round holding hands*)

Children sit in a circle and one stands in the middle. A long
string is passed through a ring and the ends are knotted. The
children hold the string in both hands so as to pass the ring
from hand to hand without showing it, while they sing the
rhyme. When they stop the child in the centre has to pounce
on the hand which she thinks holds the ring. If she finds it, she
is replaced by the holder.

Jenny at the Cottage Door

    Jenny at the Cottage door
    One two three four,
    Eating plums* off a plate
    Five six seven eight.
    O.U.T spells out.

*Must be pronounced 'plooms'.

Eena, Mena, Mina Mo

Eena, mena mina mo,
Jack a sena sina so,*
To the East, to the West,
To the old crow's nest,
Hopping in the garden,
Skipping in the sea,
If you want a pretty girl
Pray pick out she.

*Vulgar—'Sit a nigger on the po'.

I had a little moppit*
And I put it in my pocket,
And it shan't bite you

           (*repeat several times*)

But it shall bite *you*.

*From witchcraft?

For Little Children

When I was a Sailor, a Sailor, a Sailor,
When I was a Sailor, a Sailor was I,
And a this-a-way, and a that-a-way
And a this-a-way went I,

          (*Repeat the last two lines*)

All around the mulberry bush,

       the mulberry bush, the mulberry bush,

All around the mulberry bush on a

          cold and frosty morning.

When I was a Soldier . . .
When I was a Washerwoman . . .
When I was a Policeman . . .
When I was a Tailor . . .

When I was a Shoemaker ...
When I was a Lady ...

> *The first six lines walking round in file*
> *and acting the part.*

'All around the mulberry bush,' etc.

> *Take hands and dance in a ring.*

Paddy from Cork

Paddy from Cork had never been
Never before a train had seen
    He'd never seen
    The great machine
That travels along on the railway.

The last eight rhymes starting with the most puzzling Mimer one and finishing with Paddy and the railways as a novelty (now almost an antiquity), must all be Victorian, supplied by a Liverpool University student, Elsie Neale, from her father's collection. He died in 1930 and had material from his grand, and great-grandfather, of Irish origin, maternal branch, going back to 1820.

As in other cases in this section some are not, of course, purely Liverpolitan, though often a characteristic local variation occurs. As always, as with the mangle, social mores are reflected. The next sixteen are from practising teacher Lena Bergen, modest and able in an age of pedagogic self-praise and incompetence.

Mrs. Mason

Mrs. Mason broke her basin
On the way to Lime Street station
How much did it cost?
Penny, tuppence, thrippence, etc.

Here We Go Round the Mountain

Here we go round the mountain
One by one.   (*Repeat three times*)
Rise up sugar-candy,
Do a little action one by one
(*Repeat three times, children copy the action of the child
    in the centre of the ring*)
Repeat—Here we go round the Mountain
Two by two . . .

> A rosy apple, a lemon or a pear
> A bunch of roses she shall wear
> A lovely white diamond in her hair
> Choose the one to be your bride,
> Take her by her lily-white hand.
> Take her by the water,
> Give her a kiss and she'll be mine,
> She's the old man's daughter.
>
> King and queens are partners too,
> So—are—we.
> Are you ready, are you steady?
> One—two—three.
>
> Tip top toe, out you go,
> Four jolly sailor boys all in a row.
>
>> I'm on the miller's ground
>> Picking gold and silver.

Cheer, Boys, Cheer

Cheer, boys, cheer,
    My mother's got a mangle,
Cheer, boys, cheer,
    She fills it up with stones.

Cheer, boys, cheer,
    My daddy turns the handle,
Cheer, boys, cheer,
    For it nearly breaks his bones.

Spanish wine, Spanish wine,
Very very good, and very very fine.

The Pace Eggers' Devil

And on my shoulders I carry a tub.
Here comes Beelzebub?
And in my hand a frying pan
And I think myself a jolly old man.

The teacher's quote ends here. It is Beelzebub, Miss, and
the song goes on, after a Little Wit (Doctor standing by) has
stopped Bold Slasher fighting King George:

I court the lasses plenty, One by one, and two by two.
But there's none to come up to my fancy.

Some thought this purely Liverpool but of course it is not,
though do kids elsewhere use it under our steam? (Liverpudlian
Nicholas Monsarrat, in *Life is a Four-Letter Word*, seemed to
think that 'Nick, nack, paddy wack', sung by a girl in a film
representing the missionary heroine, Gladys Aylward, is
ours only. No. Doubtless I will often have to say *mea culpa*
too.) Mummers at Thurstaston, Cheshire, regularly did the
pace egg thing at Christmas till 1937, their leader, Mr. Sydney
Wilson, having the words from his grand-dad.

I Like An Apple and I Like A Pear

I like an apple and I like a pear,
I like a sailor with nice curly hair,
Oh, aye, I love him, I can't deny it,
I'll be with him wherever he goes.

He stands at the corner
On Saturday nights,
And shouts oo-ee, oo-ee
Are you coming out?
Oh aye, I love him,
I can't deny it.
I'll be with him wherever he goes.

He bought me a shawl
Of red, white, and blue,
And when we got married
He tore it in two.
Oh aye, I love him,
I can't deny it.
I'll be with him wherever he goes.

Tearing the shawl symbolic? Gypsy wedding?

Teddy Bear, Teddy Bear

Teddy bear, teddy bear, touch the ground.
Teddy bear, teddy bear, twirl right round.
Teddy bear, teddy bear, show your shoe,
Teddy bear, teddy bear, that will do.

When I Was In the Kitchen

When I was in the kitchen
Doing a bit of stitching
In came a bogey-man
And—chased—me—out.

(*Girl runs out of the rope,
another runs in quickly*)

On the Mountain Stands a Lady

On the mountain stands a lady,
Who she is I do not know,
All she wants is gold and silver,
All she wants is a nice young man,
So call in my very best friend, very best friend,
    very best friend,
So call in my very best friend
While I go out to play.

Could 'man', line 4, have been 'beau'?

Little Black Doctor, how is your wife?
Very well, thank you, she's all right.
She won't eat salt-fish,
Or a stick of licquorice.
O—U—T spells out.

All In Together to See Cinderella

When you shout your birthday
Please jump out.
January, February, March, etc. . . .
        (*Child runs out of the rope when she hears her*
                                birthday month.)

Slow down Sally
What do you like the best?
High—low—dolly—sweeper—
baby—jig . . . (*Children do actions*)

Somebody Under the Bed

I don't know who it is
I feel so very frightened
———— Mary   (*child calls someone in*)

Mary light the candle
Mary light the gas,
Go out Mary—dirty little rat.

Little Alexander Sitting on the Sand

Weeping and crying for a young man,
Rise up Sally, dry your tears,
Choose the very one you love so dear.

Raspberry, gooseberry, apple jam tart,
Tell me the name of your sweetheart.
A—B—C—D—pitch-patch-pepper.

I Call In My Very Best Friend

E. legged, I, legged, Bandy
legged   (*Girl's name*)
— Likes sugar, I like tea,
I like kissing boys—so does she.

Good-bye Mary

Good-bye Mary, while you're away
        Send me a letter
        To tell me when you're better,
Good-bye, Mary, while you're away
Don't forget your old pal—Sarah
                        and other names, each girl
                        speaks in turn, as they skip
                        round Mary)

Mary is going to the fever hospital. Though set in Manchester, Lowry's painting 'The Fever Van' is, as a postcard, a best-seller in our art gallery. And the real scene was familiar years ago. The touching song, as sung by the girls of St. Francis Xavier's, Liverpool, some of them now mothers themselves, led by Lena Bergen, to the skelp on an ashfilled playground of the rope, is one of my memories—and of the B.B.C. producer who recorded them. Now, adapted, say the Opies a 'breaking up' song.

The officials sent at night time to combat the once endemic fever in our hovels by preventing overcrowding and raided houses to see there was none—while the kids hid in outhouses, back lanes, under the bed—were called nightmen—the name given elsewhere to clearers of communal closets. The song about them, 'Little Johnny Nightman', I have mislaid. But see earlier 'Little Willy Wheelbarrow' (Chapter III).

I Had the Scarlet Fever

I had the scarlet fever,
            I had it very bad,
And if you don't believe me—
            You can go and ask me dad.

My Mother Said

George Baily of the Isle of Man, former Scouser, aged seventy-odd, recalling 'I never should play with the gypsies' etc., which, not for the first time, led from the schoolyard to the music-hall—the reverse journey, of course, not unknown also, had before the queer chorus (equivalent to my dad's general utility one 'Under the green arches, under the railways, under the green arches, under the railway') strange lines I'd not heard before—

Alpaca frock and old blind horse,
He come to a river and couldn't get across.

Where Will the Money Come From?

Mother, buy me a milking pail, a milking pail, a milking pail,
Mother buy me a milking pail, one, two, three—
Where will the money come from, the money come from, the
money come from,
Where will the money come from? One, two, three—
Pawn me father's feather bed (*repeat*) One, two, three—
Where will me father sleep, etc.,
            Sleep in the dolly tub, etc.
What will we wash in, etc.
            Wash in the thimble, etc.
What will we sew with, etc.
            Sew with the poker, etc.
What will we poke with, etc.
            Poke with your fork, etc.
What will we eat with, etc.
            Eat with your finger, One, two, three.

The young lad, in the Paddy-hat and knickerbockers, a few
months before playing with these big girlses had holidayed on
the Kerry farm belonging to the family of his friend Biddy
Doolan, who delivered the milk to his household. He knew
what a milking-can was. To the big girlses who had switched
to this game from Flinchers, Hopscotch, Maypole (dangerously
round a lamp-post using a frail rope off a discarded orange-
box) and Shop (using as money, traditionally, 'bannymug'
pieces of broken pottery found on a mud heap, as sound a
currency as any since and *pecunia non olet*) the urban refer-
ences to pawning and (the 'Pool housewives self-worked—
with a dolly peg—washing machine—about to graduate to
mixed games like I Spy and Shammy Round the Block before
I joined the big fellers in Kick the Can, Jump over Back and
Street Cricket ('six and out over the wall') were the novelties.
Odd how many features of the urban scene were missing from
the kids' minstrelsy. As in all 'folk' verse there is loving and
fighting, food and, definitely, drink. We have as much about
sailors as 'niggers' (Liverpool's then were all seamen) and

Sally. But little about docks, the river, the sea. Nothing about the Mersey Tunnel. Nothing about the great shire horses we loved, striking sparks off the cobbles as they dragged mighty loads, frighteningly running away ('get in the doorway, sis, they always run straight') having to be killed when they fell. Evacuation in the last war, when the kids at last saw milk-pails and hated them and all connected with them—unmentioned. Visits to the slaughterhouse to get bladders to play football with, flowing blood and grinning butchers. So much omitted. But who knows? We don't always know what the kids are up to.

Handy Pandy, sugar candy, which hand is it in?
Naughty Boy, you wouldn't give over——

VII

DIM RELIGIOUS LIGHT

Esau   Aaron   Moses   Dick

The First Book of Guinnesses

(i)

Holy Moses, King of the Jews,
      Bought his wife a pair of shoes;
When the shoes began to crack
      Holy Moses sent 'em back.

(ii)

Holy Moses, I am dying. Send that organman away,
Throw the tom-cat out the window
Stick some pepper up his
Holy Moses I am dying . . . etc.

(iii)

Moses
      Closes
At eight-thirty.

(iv)

The Lord said unto Moses
Come forth—And he came fifth.
—And he got the sack.—And he made a coarse apron
                        out of it.
—And he went round dashing steps.

                             Early as 1915.

A coarse, or sack, apron was worn by poor women who

'dashed' (washed) doorsteps for better-off neighbours for pennies.

> Stand up, stand up, for Jesus' sake
> The boogers at the back can't see.

No dacent Scouser but a Mancunian man (know the ould saying Manchester men, Liverpool gentlemen?) give me that, and he a publisher too. Also a few others in this book including Modern History, Chapter II.

Dearly Beloved Brethren

> Dearly beloved brethren,
>   don't you think it a sin,
> To peel the good potatoes and
> Throw away the skin?
>   The skin feeds the pig
> The pig feeds you—
> Dearly beloved brethren,
>   isn't—this—thrue?

At least seventy years old. Irish origin.

Hosanna!

>   Last night as I lay sleepin'
> There came a dream to me,
> I dreamt I saw a man getting horsewhipped in China
> For making a slide in an ice-cream saloon.
> He then wiped his feet on the shopkeeper's whiskers
> And of the cream-freezer he made a spittoon.

I don't know how my dad and his mates at their penny-a-week fitted these words to the tune. (His songs seem to have a whiskers fixation as in The Brothers Montrose whose sister mistook their hair restorer for mouth-wash and grew whiskers

on her gums.) I do know that Tommy Handley records how,
in a suburban Liverpool Band of Hope concert, his chorus
dealing with someone's rather odd trousers gained him side-
long glances—

> Who's are they, who's are they?
> They look an awful fright.

The Greatest of These?

> And though you pinched the beer
> Off the chiffonier
> It doesn't matter, dear,
> Because I LOVE YER.

—Twenties.

By God I Live

> By God I live
> By God I die,
> By God I want my penny pork pie.

Last line allegedly shouted to parson who from pulpit
announced the other two, by a little pagan, who had been lured
to service by the promise of food.—1916.

War Cry

> What do the Salvation Army run down?
>> BOOZIN' jolly well boozin'
> What do they rave about all round the town?
>> Boozin' jolly well boozin'
> They stand at the street corners, they rave an' they shout,
> They talk about tings they know nothin'* about—
> But where do they go when the lights is all out?
>> Boozin' jolly well boozin'.

Excuse the slander, Major.
*Euphemism.

Church Unity

(i)

Catty, Catty, go to mass,
Ridin' on the divil's ass.

(ii)

Proddy, Proddy, on the wall,
Penny bun to feed yiz all,
A farthin' candle to give yiz light
To read the Bible—on Sat'dy night.

See 'Out Goes She', Leslie Daber, for Dublin incidence.

Ave Maria

Holy Mary, Mother of God,
Send us down a thripenny cob—
An', for God's sake, put a bit a butter on it.

'Cob', a bread roll.

Holy, Holy, Holy

Holy, Holy, Holy,
Ten fullbacks and a goalie.

I always say there's too much defence play in soccer these days.

Jesus wept, Moses crept,
Under the bed till tea.

Sung with an over-the-shoulder glance fearing instant Divine reprisal.

Matthew, Mark, Luke and John

Matthew, Mark, Luke and John
Wid their Sundy trousers on.

THE BIG BOYSES
or Bring Back The Birch

All in together, boys,
This fine weather, boys . . .

Two Teachers Tangle

Down in the forest where nobody goes,
There lives Miss Whosthis without any clothes,
Up comes Whatsit top hat (*Oooh, ooh*) and stick,
Down comes his trousers and out comes his
    DICK fell out of the winder.
    And his mother ketched hold of his
    Dick fell out of the winder an' . . .

You are never too old to love the endless song. It was the
Headmaster of St. Malachy's, Liverpool, the late Bill Cogley,
a great advocate of such a collection as this, a most pious man,
who reminded me of this rhyme, dated by the correct clothes
for a formal visit of the male teacher whatever of the lady.
From him came 'Esau Aaron' in Chapter VII and much else.
R.I.P. He also helped with 'Morning in the Streets'.

There is a Happy Land

There is a happy land far, far away.
Oh, you should see 'em run,
When they see the butcher come,
For three slices off their bum
Three times a day.

Much of this naughtiness would seem passé to the modern teenager.

Long Before Lonnie Donegan

(A little song entitled 'When The Fields Are
White Wit Daisies There'll Be Flowers
In Scottish Homes')

My old man's a trimmer
On a Elder-Dempster boat,
He wears gorblimey trousers and
A likkle gorblimey coat.
He wears a ————— muffler,
Around his ————— throat, Cos
My old man's a trimmer on
A Elder-Dempster boat.

And

New Brighton rock,
Tuppence a block,
Twice the size of yer old feller's—
Who'll buy, WHO'LL BUY!

The Boy Stood on the Burning Deck

The boy stood on the burning deck,
His legs was full of blisters—
He had no trousers to put on so
He had to bury his sister's.

As I was saying, is Liverpool-born Felicia Heman's poem

about the adhesive boy on the burning deck the most-parodied
or is the Village Blacksmith of Longfellow?

> The muscles of his brawny arms
> Stand out like pimples on a
> Sparra's ankles?

There are so many more.

Yacki Hooley

> Yacki hooley icky doolah,
> Smack yer thingy wid a rulah.—1926.

Sex Rears

> She was a farmer's daughter
> Did what she didn't oughter,
> And got herself a son
> Because of what she done.

Recalled, sixty years after, by the former boy at a Liverpool
'ragged school,' later an Anglican vicar, now, retired, a lollipop
man.

And maybe, says Mrs. McDougall, in Ronald Frankau's
song:

> Fresh milk comes from Cowes
> And so it dam well oughter,
> You think I guess, the milk is fresh,
> But you haven't seen the farmer's daughter.

This lady, now in Hertfordshire, with her deep knowledge of
old Liverpool especially the waterfront and of music-halls, to
which children's song, all folk song, owes a big unacknow-

ledged (except mildly by A. L. Lloyd) debt, has helped greatly
with dating, but of course it can only be conjecture.

There's a hole in the middle of Nelly's white drawers.
          (*Very dramatic*)
And how do I know that my girl wears blue bloomers?
I'VE BEEN DOWN THE CELL-AR FOR COAL!

From a seventy-year old ex-Local Government worker, and
from a sixtyish schoolmaster, date themselves! Oh, the days
when short skirts and underwear were saucy.

Ighty Iddly Ighty

    Ighty iddly ighty
    Someone stole me nightie
    And I had to wear me father's shirt.

1917 from song 'Take Me Back to Blighty'.

'Without a Shirt'

These words added by kids at the end of lines in popular
songs, e.g. I was standing on the corner of the street (without
a shirt) suited our simple sense of fun. So—

    I'm the Sheik of Araby (without a shirt),
    Your love belongs to me (without a shirt)
    At night when you're asleep (without a shirt)
    Into your tent I'll creep (without a shirt)

And

    Drift with me along the shores of Minnetonka
        (without a shirt)
                      —1920's.

In the seventies my Holy Cross girls prefer to 'without etc.'
'with me boots kicking up the dust'. I suppose I'm a bit old-
fashioned!

> We're off, we're off, We're off in a motor-car
> There's fifty niggers after us
> And we don't know where we are.

As a Mick I know the best thing to do is ignore remarks not
intended to offend. Some of my best friends of course—.
One, as black as the ace of spades, Cliff, of the great Liverpool
folk group The Spinners, came to a club one night with a snow-
white poodle under his arm and he 'chortled' like the beloved
Pete of Jack, Sam and Pete in the *Marvel* years ago when I
said, 'Now, would you like her to marry a black dog'?

> The Mersey banks
> Was made for Yanks
> And little girls like Ivy,
> I'd twiddle with Ivy's flue, wouldn't you?

Tune 'Mairzy Doats'.

The Ladies, God Bless 'Em!

Here's to the gentle breezes That blow around the treeses
And Blows girls skirtses Above their kneezes
And reveal the places All men pleases
> Be Jeezus, Be Jeezus.

I was left school, and just back from a Jesuit seminary, so
when I heard this toast to the Ladies at a sixth form do, I was
deeply shocked. By the bad grammar and whiff of blasphemy.
About 1927. I have slightly altered the penultimate line.
Some, quite lost to shame, added—

> Always tidy always neat
> She made things stand that never had feet.

But Tho'

But tho' the Devil sends his wind to make the girls' skirts rise,
God is just And sends the dust
To blow in the Bad Boy's eyes.

Still

Still it's only human nature after all
To take a little girl against the wall, etc.

How the word combinations—when tights are the female
mode and fashion designer Miss Mary Quant, O.B.E., has said
'the erogenous zone is now the crotch'—rather dates the
naughty ditty.

Rough and Tumble Dick had a donkey named Mick
And that donkey couldn't half go;
It bumped its head on a lamp-post
And tumbled with its backside in the snow.

Bow Wowdler

Silence in the gallery
Order in the pit
All the little doggies
Want to have a spit.

Ev'rybody's Doin' It

Ev'rybody's doin' it,
Pickin' their nose an' chewin' it.

—1916.

The Young Democrat

Vote, vote, vote for Mister Thingy,
Throw ould Thingy in the dock,
Mister Thingy is the man
And we'll have him if we can
And we'll throw ould Thingy in the dock.

I first sang at Khaki Election and the kids' candidate lost,
a wounded soldier versus a wealthy baronet. Oh, yes, I know
kids have always sung it. But did they add 'At nine o' clock,'
when polling-stations close? Well, did they add 'By the cock'
eh?

The Wise Bachelor

There was an ould man and he had a wooden leg
He had no tobacker, No tobacker would he beg,
Another ould man Just as cunning as a fox,
He always had tobacker In his ould tobacker box.
Said one ould man, 'Will yer give us a chew?'
Said the other ould man, 'I'll be blowed if I do.
    You must save up all yer money
    And put by for the rocks
    And you'll always have tobacker in
        Yer ould tobacker box.'

May it choke him! I don't think dad, recalling it, admired
his prudence anyhow.

Honi Soit

One very hot day in summer last year
A young man was observed swimming off New Brighton Pier
He jumped in the Mersey and swam to a rock
And amused all the ladies by showing them his—
Graceful manoovers . . .

And so on, with many last minute avoidances of impropriety, going for a swim with a lady and so on until they finished the morning at a hotel by having a duck.

'Down Yonder Green Valley'

My uncle was a cobbler
With hairs just like Johnny Nobbler
And the hairs just like Johnny Nobbler
Stretched down to his knees.

Do I want a strike with a Welsh typist or the printers? You save your version till after the touch-down.

My

(i)

My poor donkey's dead, He died for the want of bread
Get a little charcoal, Stick it in his armhole*
—My poor donkey's dead.

*See previous footnote.

(ii)

My wife she died, oh, then, oh then; my wife she died,
oh then. My wife she died and I laffed till I cried
—For I knew I was single agen.
I married another, oh then, oh then, I married
another, oh then; I married another,
Far worse than the other,
And I wished I was single again.

Spanish Flu, 1918

Napoo, old thing, cheerio, chin chin, Napoo,
Take the flu. And die-ee.

Tune, Good Bye-ee.

'I Dreamt I Dwelt in Marble Halls'

I dreamt I was tickling my grandfather's fancy
With a little sweet oil and a fe-ether;
He said it was nice, So I tickled him twice and
He tickled me back wid a le-ether.

Oh, I stuck my nose Up an eleph-.

That'll do you, sonny. On yer way.

From the Chinese

Here we are
Ma
      All in a
Jam jar.
Here we are Ma
All in the one bed
All fightin' for
      The pillow.

c. 1919.

We all grew up to like nonsense sayings too, as if the ghost of tutor Lear, from Knowsley Hall, still brooded over the city—it's cold enough for a walking stick. There's a smell of broken glass. What would you rather do or go fishing?

A Matter for the Prices and Incomes Board*

If you go down Icky Picky Lane
You'll meet some dirty women,
And if you want to do 'em
You'll have to pay a shilling.
Big fat men are two pound ten
And little lads a penny.

*If it still exists when this is read.
From that debauched Manchester publisher man again.

Not THE Pill?

Lily Hill swallered a pill
Behind the chemist's door,
The chemist came out
And give her a clout
—She never went there no more.

Before the National Health Act in the days of over-busy
'penny doctors' chemists in poor areas were virtually the
medicos.

Little Miss Muffet

Little Miss Muffet sat on her tuffet,
The baby she was rockin',
A Yankee soldier had passed by
And he'd pulled up a stockin'.

Mr. Lawson of Wavertree, Liverpool, places this with
'carpet bagger' for 'soldier' in 1911 and says they sang such
parodies on the way home from Band of Hope meetings!

The boy stood on the burning deck
And did he wash his dirty neck?—
Did he 'eck!

Keating's Ode

A flea and a fly in a flue
Were imprisoned and what could they do?
Let us flee, said the fly,
Let us fly, said the flea, So—
They fled to a flaw in the flue.

(*Prestissimo*)

Revived by Liverpool folk-singer Tony Murphy composer of 'The Orange and Green.'

Remember the tin with the green label and the words 'Keating's kills fleas, moths, bugs and beetles,' a rhyme in itself? Bugs fly round in the old rhymes, picturing daily—rather, nightly, life like bums and bobbies. And bellies.

Oh My Luv——

> Roses is red, Violets is white—
> *Chorus of big boyses:* Violet's is blue.
> Roses is red, Violet's is white—
> I seen 'em on the clothes-line, Sat'dy night.

Bloomersday Again, after Drawers Day and before Knickers Night. Any rhymes *c.* 1969 about girleses' tights? The kids' cod suffragettes' slogan could now mean little. Up with the petticoats, down with the trousers.

> I love you so much, I love you so mighty
> I wish me pyjamas was next to your nighty.
> Don't be mistaken don't be misled,
> I mean on the clothes line, not on the bed.

There must be many of these Don't be mistakens coyly lingering in the 'autographs albums' of teenagers now elderly with

> Albums are red, albums are green
> But in Africa where I have been
> Albums are black.

Thirties novelist William Gerhardi used the first of the nighty verse in one of his books. Mrs. Singleton of Tyldesley, Lancs., remembered with others.

They Shouldn't Have Brought Lulu

> Lulu had a baby, she called him Sunny Jim,
> She put him in the teapot to see if he could swim.

He swam to the bottom, he swam to the top,
Lulu got excited and grabbed him by the mop.
Hey there, hey there, how about a kiss,
Shampoo and rinses, hopsies after this.

'Hopsies'?

My dearest darling ducky, I love yer clean or mucky.
Cum to me arms, my bundle uv charms,
And stick to me like putty.

Voyeur

There was a little nigger
Who never grew no bigger
So they put him in the Wild Beast Show;
He looked through a nick
And saw his Uncle Dick
Playing on his old banjo.   (*Action*)

Pussy Corner

Has anyone seen our cat?
He's got four legs and a hat.

(Good dog, Bowdler.)

You know last night, well the night before
Three tomcats come knocking at our door,
One had a fiddle, One had a drum
One had a pancake stuck to his bum.

It's either bums, bobbies, bugs or bloomers. Mrs. Wood of
Warrington one of many who reminded me.

Bernard O'Rourke of Wigan:

There was a little man
And he had a little gun

And off to the brickfields he did run
With a belly full of fat,
And a white straw hat
And (*of course*) a pancake tied to his bum, bum, bum.

'Brickfield' was 'mountains' when I was a kid in Ireland.

'A Near Thing' Said the Duke

There was a bonny Scotchman
At the battle of Waterloo,
The wind blew up his petti-coat An'
Showed his Tooraloo.

'I don't know if they frighten the enemy, they frighten me.'

The End of the School Treat

On the train or ferry or marching through the streets, tired, happy, skint, with the ha'porth of rock for Mam up the jersey, a belly full of fizzy lemonade and rock cakes the big boyses led us in:

Back home in Liverpool*
That's where I went to school,
The teacher brought me out
And give me such a clout,
I went home and told me mother
She give me another
When I got back, when I got back,
To my home in Liverpool.

*All right, some other town of three syllables ending in 'Pool. Tune, 'Back Home in Tennessee'. Mrs. Abel of Emma Hamilton's Neston now recalling it may be one of many who look back on the days when an appeal against teacher, bobby or any chastising adult brought an increased sentence. 'But I done nothing, mam.' 'Well, that'll do when you do.'

The Tatter's Song

(A genuine recollection of a real person, a tatter of course being a rag-and-bone merchant.)

> In the year nineteen ten in Litherland town
> There was an ould tatter, a regular clown,
>   He'd dance up the street
>   And he'd dance down again
> And while he was dancing, He'd sing this refrain—
>   One for yourself and one for the baby
> Ev'ry body gets two two two two,
>   Wack foi da ri do,
>   Wack fol da ri do.
> Ev'ryone gets two for one.
>   Ev'rybody gets two for one.
> Bring out yer rags, yer bottles and yer jamjars
>   Everyone gets two two two
> Ould pants of yer dad and yer grandma's shawl,
> Ev'ryone gets two for one.

Pardon Me!

> Down in the coal-hole, Diggin' up the coal—
> You can always tell a nigger by the colour of his ——
> Don't be mistaken, Don't be misled—
> You can always tell a nigger by the colour of his head.

Well, Hardly Ever

> Never throw a brick at a drownin' man
> Outside a grocery store—
> Always throw him a bar of soap—
> And he'll wash himself ashore.

c. 1900

'I gave her kisses one', the women services' version, in the 1939 war, soon permeated the top classes.—'Now it's number two,' etc., to refrain 'Roll me over, in the clover, do it again'.

Ever-ton *c.* 1930

You know the team I mean
Ten big stiffs and Dixie Dean—

From popular song 'You Know The One I Mean'.

'You'll Be a Man Before Yer Mother'

Come to yer da da, come to your da da da da da da,
Come to your dada,
Mammy put yer nicknacks back to the back
Come to yer da da da.

Langsdale Street Lullaby, twenties.

Questionable Questions

(i) D'you like salmon?—Well get a tin.
(ii) Does your mojo rise? Does your chewing gum stretch?

Unlike spearmint, mojo was a hard form of chewing gum. Personally I preferred the wax off a melting bedside candle—followed by a sip of holy water from the dusty bedroom font. Chanted questions recalled by Liverpool seaman retired in Southampton, from sixty years back. Ta, Jack.

Fits in with our screamingly witty stump speeches such as, Ladies and gentlemen, I come to address you and not to undress you—!

The Gooseberry Call

Grapes with hairs* on—
(*all together*)—Goosegogs.

*Pronounced as 'urs' as in next chant, and as in 'Murry' and 'youse t'ree is a nice purr'. A docker is nicknamed the Mangey Kitten because when told to travel by bus to another dock he says 'I haven't got me fur!' 'Pool bus conductors ask puzzled ladies from other parts for their 'furs, please'. But did not a doubtless literate official place the notice on our trams 'Treat us fairly. Travel early?'

There's Hairs On Baldy

Derisively shouted by nubile maidens after big boyses just conscious of pubescence. Adding—

Durr he is, Wheel 'im in. Bail 'im out.

That Mancunian scoffer at all things sacred, a pubic menace I call him, has

Hush, hush, whisper who dares
Christopher Robin is counting his hairs.

John Hughes Won't Save Yer

When 16-year-olds were registering for military service and it was alleged a man of that name could get you excused.

Jew Et Mon Droit

Oh me name is Solomon Levi
Keep a shop across the way—
Arra wich, arrah watt,
Arrah marraky aye.

When the tradition is oral the refrain can change and change until incomprehensible if it ever was otherwise. This is more Hibernian than Yiddish. There was a Solomon Levi, a water-front tailor, in 'Frisco, says Hugill, and the chant about him was different. Tune, 'McNamara's Band.'

We mocked the quiet old Jew peddlers, the bearded fellow with the panes of glass on his back ('Winders, winders') and could earn a penny from the orthodox switching on their gas-stoves on the Sabbath. But we liked them. There was just a giggle in our jeweller monologue:

> If you vant to buy a vatch, buy a vatch,
> If you don't want to buy a vatch, don't buy a vatch.
> But if you don't want to buy a vatch—take yer snotty nose
>   off my winder.

                                  —*c.* 1920

And our vulgar 'beautiful garden of noses, Ikey and Rachel and Moses' .

Funiculi, Funicula

> Funiculi, funicula,
> Me father was the skin uv a Spanish onion,
> And so am I, and so am I . . .

I Made You Look

> I made you look,
> I made you stare*
> I made the barber cut your hair.

*From childhood the Scouse youth has an atavistic fear of being looked at. I have been sitting quietly in an inn, not reading or making notes (I rarely join anyone), quietly contem-plating my novel or a short story, unaware of everyone about, when a truculent, self-conscious barfly lurches over and says, 'OO yew sturrin' at? Youse'll know me next time!' Of course the smart kid asked 'Who yer sturrin' at ?' replies, 'I dunno, the card's fell off.' But I am a quiet gentleman. I still have the marks to show from when I wasn't—the slight scar over one eye, the one tooth missing from all me own teeth, still recall when I was talking when I should have been listening—or running.

The Ballad of Scotty Road

The scene of the bellbottom song—which I must slightly bowdlerise, has been many places, asserts expert Stan Hugill, author of 'Sailortown and Songs of the Seven Seas', with whom Glyn Hughes and I have sung shanties to Liverpool's posh Music Society; an old sailing man himself, now Bosun of an Outward Bound School, true Scouser. But I was Scotland Road when I first heard the song, and I was thoroughly shocked. I was still in Junior school when one of the big boyses told me it as we walked, during summer holidays, round the glorious back of St. John's Market, like Paddy's Market and much more that was delightful, Waxworks, Arcade, Museum of Anatomy (with the realistic representation of the wages of sin—I am told—and the model of a real hermaphrodite), improved out of existence: that paradise of shawlies selling their potherbs and fruit, and dogs in little cages—that part I hated—and noisy cheapjacks and the heart-clinching colours of piled flowers and fruit and the competing tradesmen—'Here's a nice leg, lady.' I thought John Wigglesworth, the big boy, who also sang and get me a clip on the ear from my mother when I innocently repeated it—

> If any young lady wants a baby,
> Come to the Cock of the North

—would drop dead, there and then, among the discarded sacks and sawdust. I had been told, by the boys at the farm-camp mentioned earlier (they used to blow up the frogs with a straw in the stern, too, which made me cry) the Facts of Life but I didn't really believe them. Not in our family anyhow. When I did come to accept them I thought, as with the girl in this rhyme, first time was unlucky. John W., not met since, was reportedly still alive in 1968. Ah, but it's not a footnote, see!

> When I was a serving-girl down in Scotty Road
> My mistress she loved me, my master as well.
> One day a sailor came in from the sea.
> He asked for a candle to light him to bed.
> He asked for a blanket to lay at his head.
>   I like a fool got in to keep him warm . . .

And when she woke next morn he was about to go, with a kindly word of advice:

> If it be a daughter dance her on your knee,
> If it be a son, send the blighter* off to sea
> With bell-bottomed trousers
> And a suit of Navy blue and
> Let him climb the rigging like his old feller, etc.

*Euphemism, of course. In the thirties, a retired sailor told me that, when he was a lad in sail, he was sent to get some victuals on a Pacific Island where there was just one store. As he approached the store he could hear from inside in rum-sodden tones, 'When I was a serving-girl down in Scotty Road' and knew he was to meet a townie.

'I Blame the Mothers'

> I say, Mrs. Brown, your boy has no manners
> He sat on my doorstep and left two big bananas.

Strange Ambition

> O if I had the bulk of an elephant
> And a trunk about ten inches long
> I would climb to the heights of oblivion (!)
> And spit on the people below.

No prize, as old comics used to say, for spying the three euphemisms.

Moon Rock

Just to show it is still going on the lollipop man tells me the top class marched across round time of first moon landing chanting:

> Baby Baby Astro
> Daddy's gone so fasto
> To find a little space skin
> To wrap the Baby Astro in.

What Is It?

> It bursts the stitches
> Of little boys' breeches
> And sets forth peas.

1920. Breeches recur as often as teacher with the Big Fat Cane which dusted them.

Both sad in their way are two from Mrs. Gammidge of Bolton:

> There's many a ship been lost at sea
>   For want of tar and rudder;
> There's many a feller lost his girl
>   For walking out with anudder.

> A man walked on the railway line
> The driver heard a squeal,
> The porter took an oily rag
> And wiped him off the wheel.

Who Was It?

> Oh, where did you get the soap for your lather
> And who cut the hair off the man with the wig,
> What was you at when you shampoo'd the cat,
> Was it you or your father who shaved the pig?

Mrs. Smith, Sheffield.

Be a Good Boy Now

Don't throw the lamp at father,
It's a shame to waste the oil.
(*Chorus:* Darrah, and the same to you?
Roscoe, you made a mess of me . . .)

Twenties, last line added at time of Fatty (Roscoe) Arbuckle
trials after death at party of actress Virginia Rappe.

Seriously Though

Mrs. Wooley assures me children sang this sad song, as they
surely sang, about the same time the 'raggety sailor boy'
(Chapter 2) suddenly (1970) revised:

Mother, come bathe my forehead
I'm growing very weak,
Just a little drop of water
Pour upon my burning cheek;
Mother, go tell my playmates that I never more will play.
Give them all my toys but—mother—
Put my little shoes away:
Santa Claus—he brought them to me
With a lot of other things
And—I thought I saw an angel—
With a pair of silver wings.

Glyn Hughes is putting this to music. Words copyright as
are all in book.

To An Eavesdropper

There was an old woman
And she could do—
Kiss me bum
And so can you.

1900

Reply to 'I Thought—'

You know what thought did?
Followed a muck-cart
And thought it was a wedding.
Or Wet himself and thought he was sweating.

The Cause of the Strike

(To be sung near Cammell Laird's gates.)

Dockyard maties children, sitting on the dockyard wall
Just like their fathers—Doing damn-all.
Soon they'll be grown up and be dockyard maties too
Just like their fathers—Damn all to do.

'Damn-all' is a euphemism of course.

Down In Brownlow Gardens

Down in Brownlow Gardens,
The game is never slack,
And a fella once went solo on
Ace King Queen Ten Jack.

Take My Money, Take My Life

Take my money, take my life,
Take my starvin' kids and wife
But (*most pathetical*) don't put my fa-ather's whiskers
up for sale.
Patter: Take me life and save me money for me old age.

A Proper Tearaway

There was a young girl of Ohio
Who used to slide down the banister stairs,

When she thought no one was nigh her;
One day her brother Josiah,
On the banisters placed some barbed wi-er—
    It wouldn't be best,
    To tell you the rest, but—
The flags are half-mast in Ohio.

Had its vogue among us in the early twenties, with saucy but short-lived limericks, like 'The Young Man of St. Paul's Who Used to Do Stunts on the Halls'. This one could have been brought home by an older brother Cunard or White Star.

Boy Scout's Trumpet Call

And you won't go to heaven when you die, Mary Ann,
    When you die, Mary Ann,
    You won't go to heaven when you die.

So

To Bed to Bed

To bed, to bed, said Sleepy Head.
                  Time enough, said Slow.
Put on the pan,
    said Greedy Guts
        And we'll have some Scouse before we go.

Shrill voice off :
        Get up them stairs
        Remember I'm your mother (*fade out*)
        Till yer father gets another.

THAT'S ALL THAT'S IN IT.

INSTEAD OF A PREFACE
or A Footnote to End All Footnotes

It is instead of a thesis really. A Holmesian monograph was projected. I wanted to go well beyond the notes and trace the sources of Liverpool Children's Rhymes. But suppose I could write it, who would read it?

I boiled down what I had to say besides the notes, after a lifetime study of the rhymes, to a preface. But after the excellent foreword who would want a preface? You wanted to get to the main matter.

I thought also of an appendix—maybe two. I had more to say about the kids' games. Many points needed expanding. But who ever reads an appendix? In a book it has as little value as in a body.

Superfluous lags the writer on the page.

You have had the result of my fifty years collecting, I had already given maybe an intolerable deal of prose bread of my own when you wanted only the intoxicating sack of other people's verse.

(I had thought of giving you some of my own, Modern Scouse Nursery Rhymes like

> 'Little George Melly
> Went to the Delly
> For a pudden on Christmas Eve,
> He stuck in his thum
> And pulled out a plum
> And the headwaiter asked him to leave.'

> Or 'The wife of a docker
> Went to the locker

To get the poor booger a bevvy;
When she got there
She found it was bare
'Cos the ale had been nicked by his nevvy.')

Yet I could not drift away though the curtain was coming down and nobody has shouted Author—not really author anyway—without covering three points as even the most modern bathing-dress (fem.) must. Two are about the book. The third about those without whose alliance the book could not have been compiled filling a long-felt want—mine.

1 (a) So much of the old Liverpool is passing, daily some rusty or barnacled relic of the dirty old seaport is bulldozed into rubble to be replaced by something making Liverpool look no different from Leeds or Birmingham. The outward signs of brave, wry humour of an idiosyncratic people, themselves facing all those forces working for uniformity go one by one. Something of their spirit must be recorded before it is too late. To provide a footnote in future social history for posterity, if any. The spirit is nowhere better reflected than in these songs, already being forgotten.

Liverpool is not unique I—reluctantly—admit; it has some affinity with other seaports and British cities. But it had many differences and to me all differences are worth protecting, national or local, while we strive for world unity politically, complete brotherhood spiritually. Let us preserve oddity, let us cherish variety, foster the non-centric, realise what Ivor Brown called the 'importance of being parochial'.

1 (b) Some of the songs are not even Liverpool's sole property, I would have to confess on my deathbed. But I would come back from the grave to say that when there are twins they are not identical. And if they look identical—the Liverpool one was born first. Our heritage has been preserved nationally by the incomparable Opies. I deliberately did not re-read them or personally consult them, as I am sure I could, while compiling this collection so that I could make my assertion without contradiction. Well, suppose there is a teechy rhyme here or there someone might have had before us

—you can get stewed mutton and veg and spuds and potherbs outside Liverpool, I am told; it would never taste the same as Scouse, it would not possess that Jenny Sez Kwah, the wacker's cordon bleu, the accolade, 'yew cud throt a mouse across it'. Don't forget it takes a Scouser nose to sing a Scouser song through. Like Shakespeare we gloriously transmute when we pinch.

1 (c) Perhaps I am temerarious too when I assert that almost all these rhymes, surely a majority of them, have not seen print before. (Like my own

> 'Tom, Tom, the docker's son,
> Stole a sheep that's what he done.
> But, when he too worked at the docks,
> He drove 'em through the gates in flocks.'

Or 'Umpty Scouser sat on a rail
> Watching the ships into Arringtin sail;
> All the Queen's foreman
> And all the Queen's men
> Cudden get Umpty to go in the pen,'

the pen being the employment hall at Queens and other docks.)

The source is oral and proletarian. The city and town worker like his rural predecessor in folk-song and the shanty-singing sailor and the itinerant worker like the navvy couldn't write 'em down if he would. And when earnest academic types came to write them down they missed much, they bowdlerised much and much was not given to them from that secretiveness the so-called lower classes and all children always use with their bosses and so-called betters, this is their's why give it to you? It is the only sort of thrift the penniless can practise, the weak's defence. It is also an instinct to resist anything said being taken down and used in evidence against (as my class must always interpret the bobby's caution) and being conde-scended to, cajoled, patronised. You don't know everything, Lord Muck. God knows, mate, and He won't snitch. Shut up, here's Miss. Some of the compilers were simply kidded. An Irish parish priest once told me of a knickerbockered type from Trinity who penetrated the Gaeltacht and returned spluttering excitement with *Tarrara boom de ay*.

Maybe as with the shanty, the harvest paean, the slum kids' marching song, the skipping and counting chants, one must accept a written version could have existed before the oral tradition was initiated, as hymns (like the 1914–18 trench songs sung by a generation who had been regular attendants at Sunday school), parodied, often as music-hall songs. I know that of some herein, especially my father's lullabies. About 1912 the Pelissier Follies used the 'My old man's a fireman On the Elder Dempster boat' which turned up, renovated, again in a Lonnie Donegan fifties show but it already existed orally in a franker version than Pelissier used, as a very old E.D. fireman, one of the last, Joe Timpson, insists.

The often execrable rhymes I take to be evidence of oral birth but not coercive.* The eye does not correct the ear when the child hazards a written rhyme, I have found, and written nursery rhymes often are bad too, even sophisticated ones which probably appeared first only in print (in hornbooks and Mother Goose and such which must, however, have included oral-born). Even the work of literate (?) writers of popular songs like the creator of the mammy-song of the twenties 'I Love That Dear Old Lady': 'she meets you half-way Half-way up the pathway, That's half-way to heaven— and home'.

It doesn't really matter. All herein were street songs and street songs on Merseyside in my own recollection or the memory and observation of reliable informants. (I'm no knickerbockered University type I assure you.)

2 (a) Need I before getting to my third part, dealing with those informants, defend this honest compilation from the naughtiness the honesty demands and which, to my mind, is as innocent as the soldier's reasons for singing that he loved his wife or the frank and aching human sexuality of some of

* I give some examples on p. 131.

the shanties. I detest filth in private talk, on TV, in art, or literature.

Max Miller and the Edwardian music-hall artistes, Donald McGill and the comic seaside postcard, the Pink 'Un writers were countrymen of Chaucer's Miller, Bottom, Hogarth who would have spat at some of the pornography-purveying pimps so often mincing across our stages and screens, sniggering through our Sunday papers, leering as prize-winners from the walls of our art galleries with their phallic obsession. The kids' *piddle* and *bloomers* and even *bugs* are clean and honest and harmless and English.

There is of course as I recently pointed out in an essay published by *Sphinx*, the Liverpool University Guild mag., a little self-consciousness in the kids' use of some noa words (as we anthropologists call them), *verboten* expressions behind the back of authority—parent, teacher, bobby—half hopeful of being, yet fearful of being, overheard. 'This sort of stuff'— teacher's coy euphemisms for the kids' candid cloacisms— 'perpetuates the dichotomy in all our minds between what is not allowed in the classroom and "parley" in the back entry, a preview and warning of hypocrisy, two-facedness, chicanery, pedantry, prudishness, political forked tongues which is so much of the adult life.' So—'In the fourth class bum's the word'. We will never be so naughty or so innocent again.

Home may join the school in forming two worlds for the child. It comes with slum-clearance to cold remote unfriendly suburbs, running water, electricity and Maggie getting a job with a pools firm and forcing granny to discard her ould shawl and call the lobby the hall, the parlour the lounge, replacing good English words with false genteelisms. S——house, closet, 'the back', lavat'ry, toilet, loo, powder room.... Wackers of the world unite! S—— on all gentility, balls on the mealy-mouthed.

Folk-song, for adults or children, is naturally older than big towns and rural life tends to what the first compilers thought coarse. In the town for the poor, the only source of folk-song, lack of privacy, the young's close contact with adults, does not make for reticence. *It's yewr bad mind*, the slummy's uncon-scious translation of the Garter motto, is all.

Fashion expert Mary Quant says the crotch is now the erogenous zone as if, whatever the competition, it had ever ceased to be.

Bum and *dick* and other parts of the zone, associated with *bloomers* and *flies* and *shirts*, were almost asexual in the kids' world, urinating and defecation and the water/earth closet being summoned up rather than copulation—and the bed was associated with the bug, though both words they cunningly guessed upset the clean-necked spinster at the blackboard, because these were things to be concealed and their revelation offensive to the elder.

Up to the adolescent age which of course these days may be earlier as big boyses and girlses get bigger earlier every year. But many men are boys all their lives and many of them getting their 'senior citizen' pension can giggle into their beer on stag night at the workingmen's club when the band sweeping into *Orpheus in the Underworld* leads to a row of high-kicking boiling-pieces revealing frilly and not very white drawers. For most it passes like goosing, 'have you for the highest' and self-abuse. It has for sure nothing of the innate wickedness of the humourless painstaking pornography of the *soi-disant* permissive age.

One thing the naughtiness seems to prove to me. How much of the mass of surviving rhymes was orally passed on. The naughtiness would not have been written down in those days. Myself am so much of an earlier age that I, with no evil intent, merely a desire to give a true record, have had to suppress, I felt, here and there.

2 (*b*) Worse, some might think, is the insensitivity of using the word 'nigger" as we kids did. Naïve, not insensitive, which also tends to prove oral transmission: the written word is never as simple as the oral and many of us hesitate to put on paper, for all to see, things, meaning no harm, we say when we can pick our hearers.

In the text I glanced at this subject rather nervously: I have two sons who have worked at 'mixed' youth camps in U.S.A. to whom the word—mispronunciation of the old French-

Spanish word for black—is more offensive than a big, big Eff.
I can see the point.

Yet I don't mind if you call me Whitey or Blanco—though
Reddy would be more correct (all negroes are not black). You
say, 'Ah, it is a sign of subjection, of contempt'. No race or
religion has been more reviled than mine but I get a sense of
superiority, a conviction of my own rightness, when fools
attack either.

Negroes who achieve position, power, wealth, are still
absurdly touchy. I have achieved none of these things, have
never had a car, a house, a dinner suit or an expensive holiday.
I have, one way and the other, met many important and rich
people; I have never had intimacy with any. My education was
paid for by a charitable lady whose name I don't know. In the
middle of the last war I was not earning £5 a week. Fairly well
known for 30 years as writer and entertainer I have never
thereby averaged more than £300 a year. Yet you can call me
what you like so long as you don't call me too early in the
morning.

As an African missionary of many years service to a flock
that loved him said to me, 'When, like us Micks and old Ikey
over there, they can laugh at themselves—then they are
emancipated!' Changing 'Ten Little Nigger Boys' to 'Ten
Little Golliwogs' and finding even that did not suit the Race
Relations Board's West Midlands Conciliation Committee
dealing with the ladies of Gentleshaw and Cannock Wood
Women's Institute, Staffs. 'You equate coloured people with
golliwogs', chairman Mr. Otto Hahn.—*Daily Express*, April
13, 1970—is absurd, like the Zionist who is more nationalistic
than Hitler.

It is just naïvety, there is no malice. We loved our golliwogs
as our dads loved the nigger minstrels.

2 (*c*) Naïvety too is the source of the intense beauty of some
of the girls' skipping rhymes. The street has become again a
country field and we leave the mangles and nightmen and
pawnshops and pub doorstep vigils—
        '*All in a bokkle o gin, All out a bokkle a stout*'
for Sally with the blue ribbon and a beloved sailor boy, the

miller's ground, the hammer on the block and a great big ship going through the alley-o.

We seem to be back in the gay infancy of the world, to have found for a moment our lost garden.

For a moment. . . . It is the most evanescent of beauties but, in a way, it lasts us till the day we die. That is why, when compiling this book, I could find so many helpers among the elderly. How often have I said thank Heaven for little old girls!

When I found children who recalled the old rhymes I almost invariably found grandma in the shadows round the hob. This is truer of the working class because mam, maybe perforce at work all day, so often delegates her maternal duties to *her* mam. The natural anarchy of the child finds age ready to co-operate.

So, when it comes to acknowledgment it is the old girls I bow to first. Then the teachers, especially at Holy Cross school which is in a slum area, with children looking and speaking as, clean, intelligent and good-mannered, as well as any in the finest-appointed school in the kingdom.

Many of the poems in this book came of course from teachers as the text indicates. A selection of the contents of this book appeared in 1969, printed in Liverpool, for folk round Merseyside. There were only about a thousand copies but it penetrated much of the North Country, the base remaining Scouseport.

Bill Grundy on a Saturday morning for the BBC from Manchester played recordings of Liverpool kids picked at random outside my Huyton Council house singing the old songs while they skipped—and Bill delighted in a reference to the 'skelp' of the rope, though to get this at its best dockside cobbles are needed.

There followed public attention in the Northern edition of the *Sunday Mirror* and hundreds of rhymes poured into the paper some, over a period of three weeks, being printed therein. The rest the ever-helpful Editor sent to me and after using some suitable to the purpose of this book the best of the rest were passed on to the Opies who have a number of local files of the same sort covering much of the U.K. I must thank Mr. Conron and his readers very much. Many I have written to.

It would not be possible to name all herein though many are given credits in the text.

But I must report that the best came from ageing ladies. And the older the ladies the naughtier the things they recalled. I found this was the case also when I spoke to various women's organisations on the subject.

The most interesting meeting however, that I attended, though the material supplied by my listeners was not immediately useful, was all male, most of them this side of forty, at 'that Grand Institution, Walton Hotel' (as my father sang). Thank you Father Atherton and screws and inmates of Her Majesty's Prison, Walton, Liverpool.

There is much repetition—more than half of the correspondents recalled the old rhyme about Queen Caroline which became 'Dan, Dan the Dirty Old Man' but other rhymes recurred frequently, probably Doctor Foster being second to Dan. Most had different versions from mine and some writing could be quite nasty about that, comparing my text and what they recalled with all the caustic comment of one Biblical or Shakespeare commentator to another. I wondered whether this was Anty Nelly or the Dead Sea Scrolls.

Sign of affection retained for years, proof again of oral transmission.

The best helpers are named in the text. Those who aren't must accept a gratitude to them as profound as to those named. My gratitude is mainly for being instructed in the variations which I'd love to record some day in a bigger, deeper work. I honestly received little wholly new from most correspondents. Two-thirds of this book, I would venture, come from my father, myself, and Glyn Hughes.

Though he is named in the text I must close with a special mention of Glyn. But I am sure he would let me pause for a moment while I give you another Merseyry Rhyme:

> 'Rock a bye, baby, on the treetop
> When the wind blows the cradle will flop.
> —Wouldn't you think its flippin mam
> Would have more sense and buy a pram ?'

Glyn Hughes, son and grandson of Welsh clergymen, is

everything I'm not: young, goodlooking, world-travelled, a clever musician, unmarried. But we both went to school in Liverpool and, getting our livings for many years outside it, love Liverpool and we both have good memories; we also have scores of Scouse friends on Merseyside and *in partibus infidelium* whose hearts are still in Scotty Road, who remember thee, O Liver-bird. A great companion is Glyn, but a loner, we may meet almost daily for months then he's off on the tober. At present we are running a Scouse Museum and composing Liverpool songs after his world success with 'Whisky on a Sunday'. 'Crooked Lane' just recorded will be followed by 'Commutation Row', 'The Tuppeny Doss' and 'My Old Grannie's a Shawlie'.

But now we are off to a free-and-easy where, after our turn, the self-appointed 'churman' will lead the chant:

> 'A jolly good song, jolly well sung,
> Cheers for the singuh, every-one,
> If youse can beat it You're welcome to thry—
> But please to remember the singuh is dhry!'

Which will be soon put right. Tarrah well.

F.S.

THEY SOUND ALL RIGHT: Some Bad Rhymes

Alas, flat; bananas, pyjamas; bananas, manners; blarney, Army; bum, gun; bum, run; cat, back; cotton, bottom; cried, size; Delly, penny; fire, higher; fire, Jeremiah; fire, liar; flop, off; garden, farthings; God, cob; gun, come; horse, across; jug, above; kipper, knickers; kitchen, stitching; line, overtime; mangle, handle; mendin', send him; minister, vinegar; Ohio, nigh her; pepper, better; pocket, got it; putty, mucky; shovel bubble; sofa, poker.

BIOGRAPHICAL NOTE ON THE AUTHOR

FRANK SHAW has written a good deal and appeared before the public a good deal and, in both capacities, is very versatile. But his work, at least in the last twenty years, has been usually about Liverpool in some form or other. In everything he writes nowadays you'll find some reference to Liverpool, especially its unique adenoidal dialect Scouse, which he speaks fluently through his own nose. 'I've been writing since I was a school-boy fifty years ago—don't know when I didn't write, wrote a play at ten, a hymn to the Trinity before that, had poems in print in my teens. But my first stuff in print was when I was eleven, in *St. Francis Xavier's College Magazine*. I was writing about Scouse then, with, believe it or not, the uncle of Peter Moloney my rival in the Scouse industry—though I was the first in it. But for twenty years I wrote about history, politics, short stories set elsewhere and never mentioned the dear old 'Pool.'

Father of four, granddad of six, he recently retired from H.M. Customs. 'I worked full-time for them for forty years while being a part-time writer. Unkind superiors put it the other way about. Now I'm a full-time writer.' He also performs regularly for Radio Merseyside and is making records; he has done TV work, for both sides, and expects to do a deal more in the future, writing and performing. Probably with Denis Mitchell for whom he did his first broadcast with Bessie Braddock, Arthur Askey, and other Liverpudlians for Liverpool Civic Week, 1951; later with Mitchell and cameraman Roy Harris he shared the Italia Prize for the year's best documentary, the BBC's *Morning In The Streets*, set mainly round Dingle, Everton, Scotland Road, and featuring schoolchildren at play.

His last three books, written in association with others, *Oxtail Book of Liver Verse*, *Lern Yerself Scouse* ('best title I ever created'), *Gospels In Scouse* (which was also recorded) carry the Liverpool theme this book does. But before them he wrote the standard *Court Procedure For Customs Officers* (he was Publicity Officer for the Customs officials' union). From 1967–1969 he held the annual award for the Civil Service Writer of the Year, the Matthew Finch Silver Cup. He has written for a variety of periodicals, here and in the U.S.A., from *New Statesman* to the *Prescot Reporter*, Liverpool University's *Sphinx* to *Billy's Weekly Liar*. He even smuggled Scouse into the august pages of *Punch*, appearing for two years running, in the annual *Pick of Punch*. Has worked for the Central Office of Information and Canadian Broadcasting.

He also wrote the Unity Theatre play, in Scouse, *The Scab*, ran the *Pot of Scouse Review* at the Everyman in 1967, has been a local councillor, school governor, club performer, patron of War on Want, Jesuit novice, and, at the very beginning, a little lad in Tralee. 'A long journey, I hope to go much farther but my heart will always be round the back streets of the 'Pool.' That is why he made for the port's posterity, if any, with actor Jack Gordon of Unity, the recordings of Liverpool customs and speech—now in the City archives.

Although (he says) 'slung out of the church choir—for miming' he has appeared at Fritz Spiegl's Scouse-and-Strauss concerts; on the sacred podium of the Liverpool Philharmonic he smoked a cigar and shared a bottle of stout with Stan Kelly (author of *Liverpool Lullaby*, etc.) while reading the *Liverpool Echo*. With fellow-'singer' Glyn Hughes he is currently running the Scouse Museum, a perfectly serious project with some unique exhibits like the Aintree Iron and a 'purr' of docker's boots. (What's special about docker's boots?—'They get sweatier!')

'Glyn and I' (writes Frank) 'as composers of local songs and, very rarely in my case, performers and as writers are perfect partners though two very different persons. But we both love Liverpool, both went to school there, are totally anti-bourgeois though quite conventional. He stands at a bar and I love to sit. We have Liverpool and working-class friends all over the world. He has had twenty jobs, I was a civil servant nearly forty years. Both of us dreamt of a book like this and we are now collecting adult street rhymes. Stand back!'

In 1947 Frank was one of the British delegation to the

International Town-planning Congress at Hastings. In 1968, at Warwick University, for a thesis proving that Shakespeare was a Scouser—and because Stan Kelly was a member of the faculty—Frank received the honorary degree of M.Sc. (Master of Scouse). He gives talks to youth clubs, townswomen's guilds, pensioners, Rotary and Noel, and the lads in the Blue Boar lounge, Huyton. He has been chairman of a youth club, a working men's club, a literary club, a bowls club. 'I have set a *New Statesman* competition, judged a Miss Liverpool contest, read the lessons in a Prodessan cherch, and I am a fully paid-up member of Michael Barsley's Left-handers' Association.' All this and a serious student of linguistics, as witness a long series in the *Lancashire Dialect Magazine* and 'Why We Speak That Way' in the *Saturday Book* 1967.

'I can't swim, ride a bike, mend a fuse, or fasten my shoe-laces.' Frank is half-way through a book about food and drink on Merseyside, *The Bevvy Cook*, but intends to complete his autobiography first, *The Confessions of a Left-handed Customs Officer*. He is also working with Alan Watts, Editor of *The Civil Service Author*, on a book about twenties–thirties 'things'—from spats to spittoons, chamberpots to trouser-presses, called provisionally *I Like Liquorice Laces*.